HOW TO DRAW CHIBI

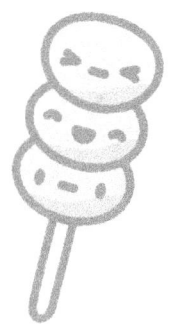
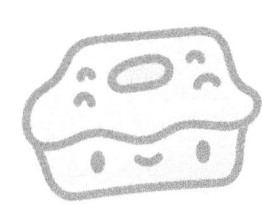
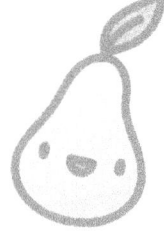

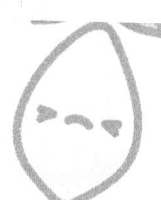
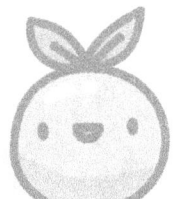
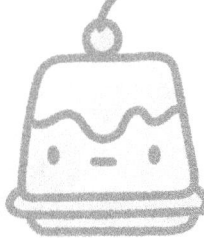
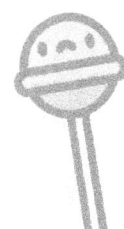
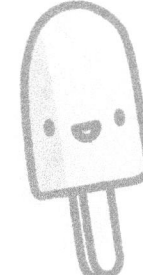
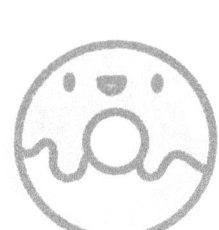

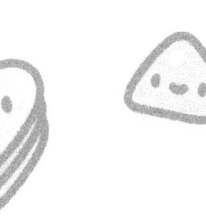
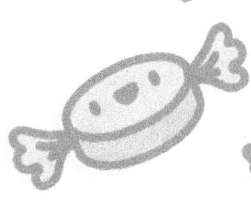

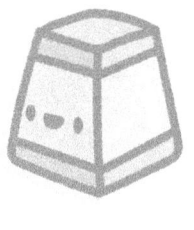

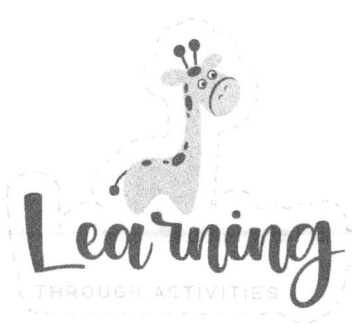

© Copyright 2021 - All rights reserved.

The content contained within this book may not be reproduced, duplicated or transmitted without direct written permission from the author or the publisher.

Under no circumstances will any blame or legal responsibility be held against the publisher, or author, for any damages, reparation, or monetary loss due to the information contained within this book, either directly or indirectly.

Legal Notice:
This book is copyright protected. It is only for personal use. You cannot amend, distribute, sell, use, quote or paraphrase any part, or the content within this book, without the consent of the author or publisher.

Disclaimer Notice:
Please note the information contained within this document is for educational and entertainment purposes only. All effort has been executed to present accurate, up to date, reliable, complete information. No warranties of any kind are declared or implied. Readers acknowledge that the author is not engaged in the rendering of legal, financial, medical or professional advice. The content within this book has been derived from various sources. Please consult a licensed professional before attempting any techniques outlined in this book.

By reading this document, the reader agrees that under no circumstances is the author responsible for any losses, direct or indirect, that are incurred as a result of the use of the information contained within this document, including, but not limited to, errors, omissions, or inaccuracies.

SPECIAL BONUS!

Want These 2 Books For FREE?

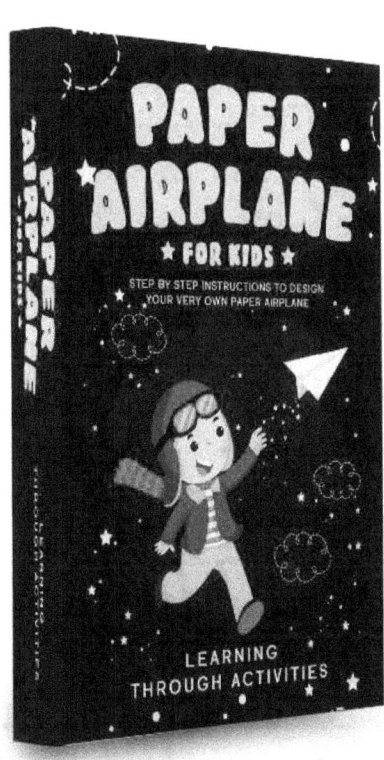 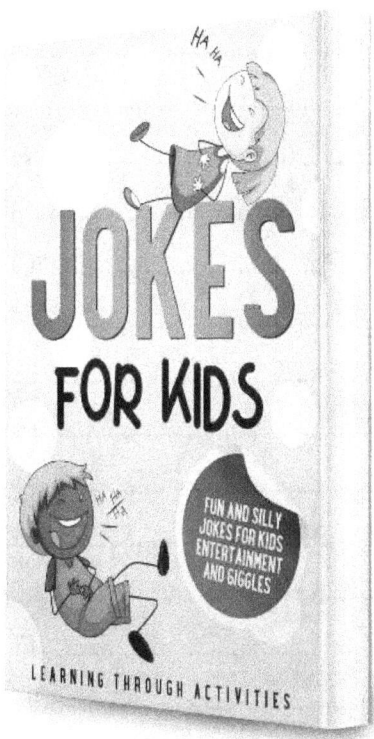

Get **FREE**, unlimited access to these and all of our new kids books by joining our community!

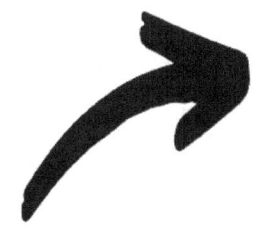 

Scan W/ Your Camera To Join!

CONTENTS

INTRO	4	BEAKY	31
EYES	5	GIRLY	32
TUMBLY	6	SHELBY	33
TEEBEE	7	DRIFTER	34
BOUNCE	8	ROB	35
CONNIE	9	CORN-PIE	36
CURL-TOP	10	MILKO	37
CEE-CEE	11	BOTTBEE	38
SUNSHINE	12	SPRITE	39
SWEETY	13	CRUMBIE	40
TIGS	14	CHUTIE-CUTIE	41
ANTIPODES	15	DUDE	42
SNIG	16	GREEN TIP	43
SPEEDY	17	SLURP	44
RATTUS	18	DASH	45
SQUISH	19	SPLASH	46
DOTTY	20	SWISSY	47
MONKEM	21	LEGGY	48
MOOGIE	22	PUNG	49
FINNSTER	23	BOXY	50
FLAP	24	SPROUT	51
SAURY	25	CHEEPER	52
FLIT	26	CHUM	53
SCAT	27	SWIRL	54
SKIP	28	NOO-NOO	55
DOLLY	29	CONCLUSION	56
SNUGS	30		

INTRODUCTION

WELCOME TO 'HOW TO DRAW CHIBI.' THIS BOOK IS FULL OF ALL DIFFERENT KINDS OF FUN, CUTE CHARACTERS! YOU'LL BE AN ARTIST BEFORE YOU KNOW IT!

EACH CHIBI HAS EASY TO FOLLOW INSTRUCTIONS THAT WILL STEP-BY-STEP HAVE YOU DRAWING THEM LIKE A PRO!

NOT ONLY WILL YOU LEARN HOW TO DRAW ALL OF THESE CHIBI CHARACTERS, YOU WILL ALSO LEARN WHERE EACH OF THEM LIVE AND WHAT THEY LOVE!

PLEASE DON'T WORRY IF YOUR CHIBI CHARACTERS TURN OUT A LITTLE DIFFERENT FROM THE ONES IN THE PICTURES, WE ALL HAVE OUR UNIQUE STYLE, AND ALSO, PRACTICE MAKES PERFECT!

GENERALLY, IT'S BEST TO START WITH A PENCIL WHILE YOU ARE GETTING THE HANG OF IT, SO LITTLE MISTAKES CAN BE EASILY ERASED. THEN MOVE ONTO PENS, COLORED, SPARKLY, WHATEVER YOU LIKE.

HAVE FUN!

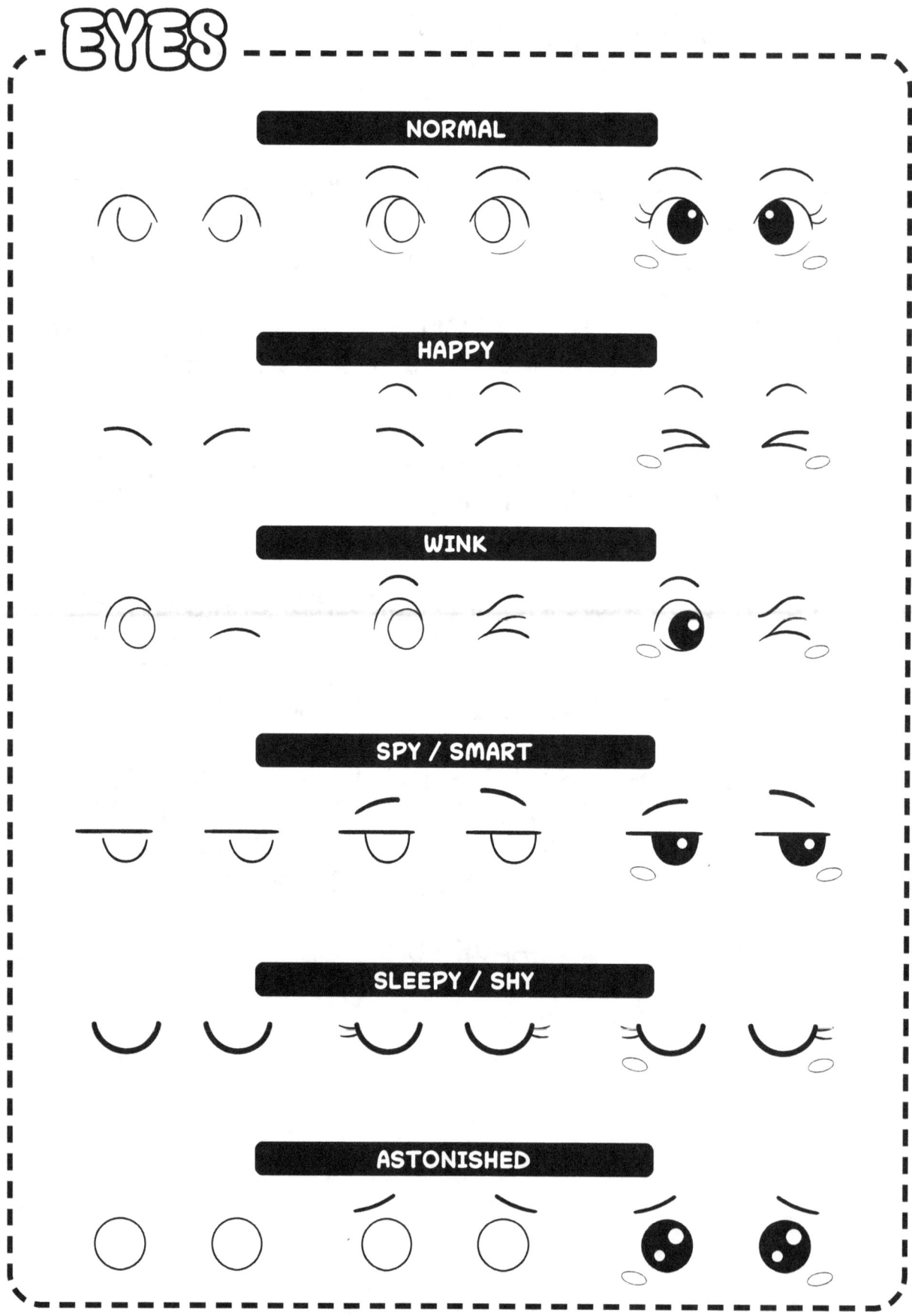

TUMBLY

LIVES: IN AN ENGLISH ZOO, AND IS SO SPOILED.

LOVES: PLAYING WITH ANTS, BUT IS AFRAID OF SQUISHING THEM!

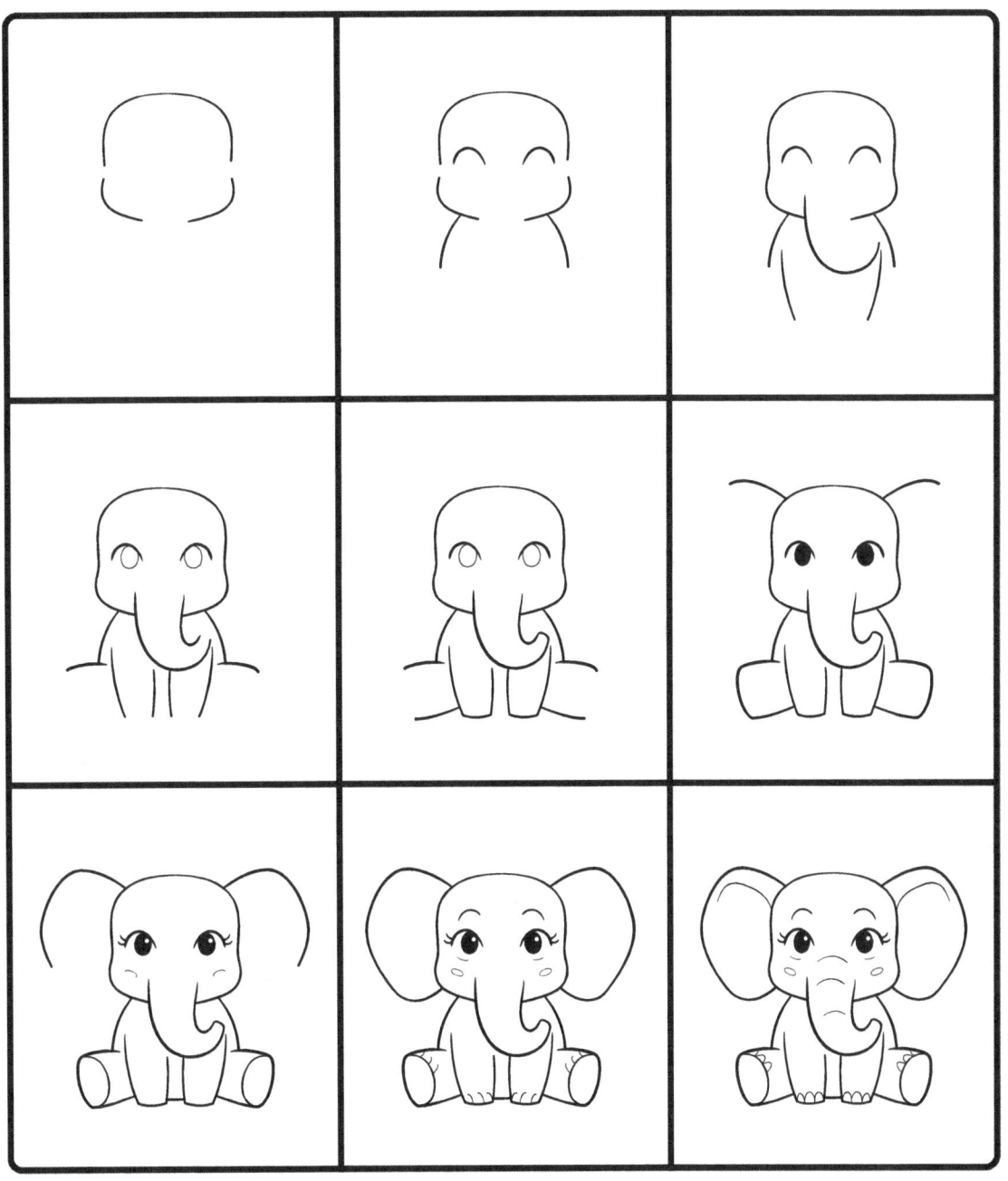

HOW TO DRAW DINOSAURS

TEEBEE

LIVES: IN A LITTLE GIRL'S BEDROOM IN A CABIN IN THE WOODS.

LOVES: THE WOODS, BUT IS NOT A REAL BEAR AND SO IS ALWAYS STUCK INSIDE.

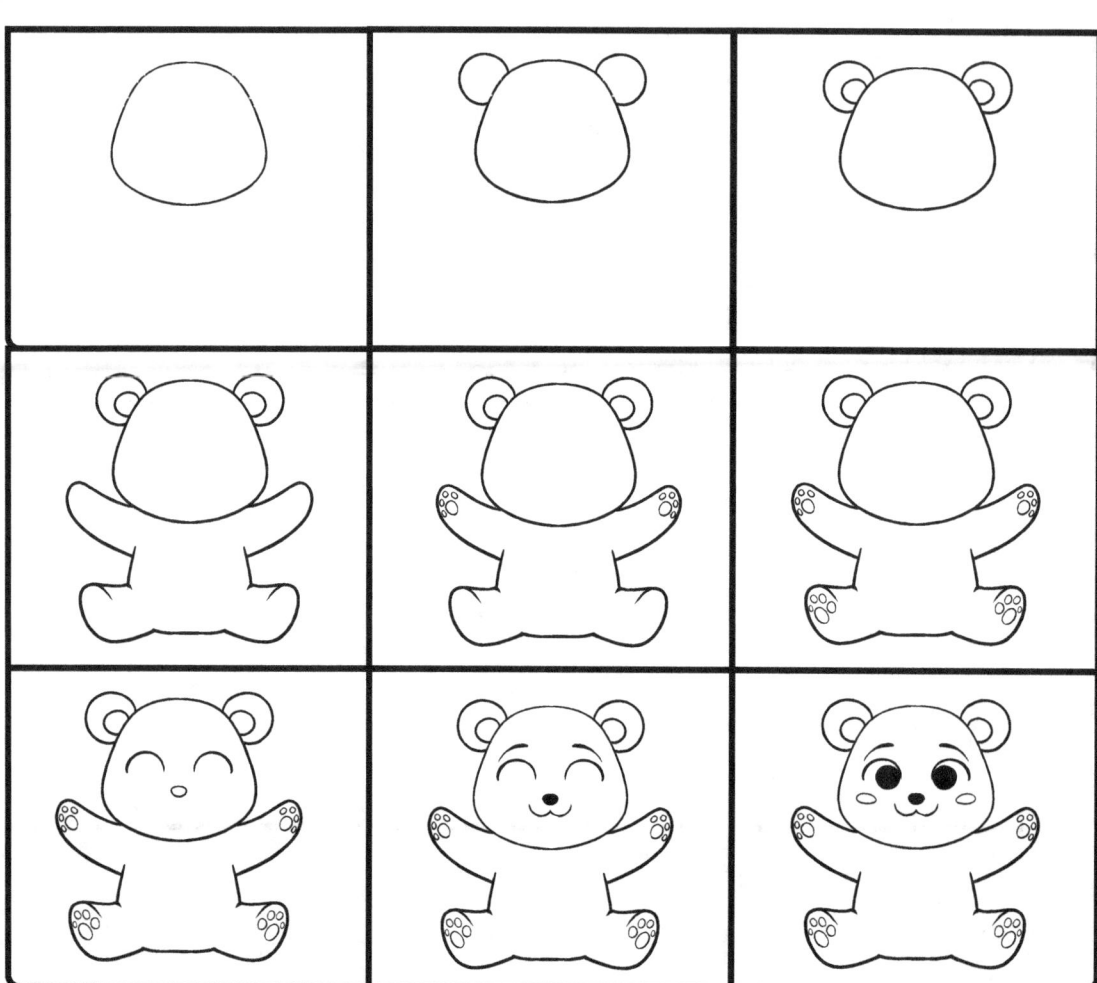

HOW TO DRAW DINOSAURS

BOUNCE

LIVES: WITH A YOUNG FAMILY AND THEIR SILLY CAT.

LOVES: ROLLING IN THE DIRT AFTER A BATH, BUT HE ALWAYS GETS IN TROUBLE, WHY?

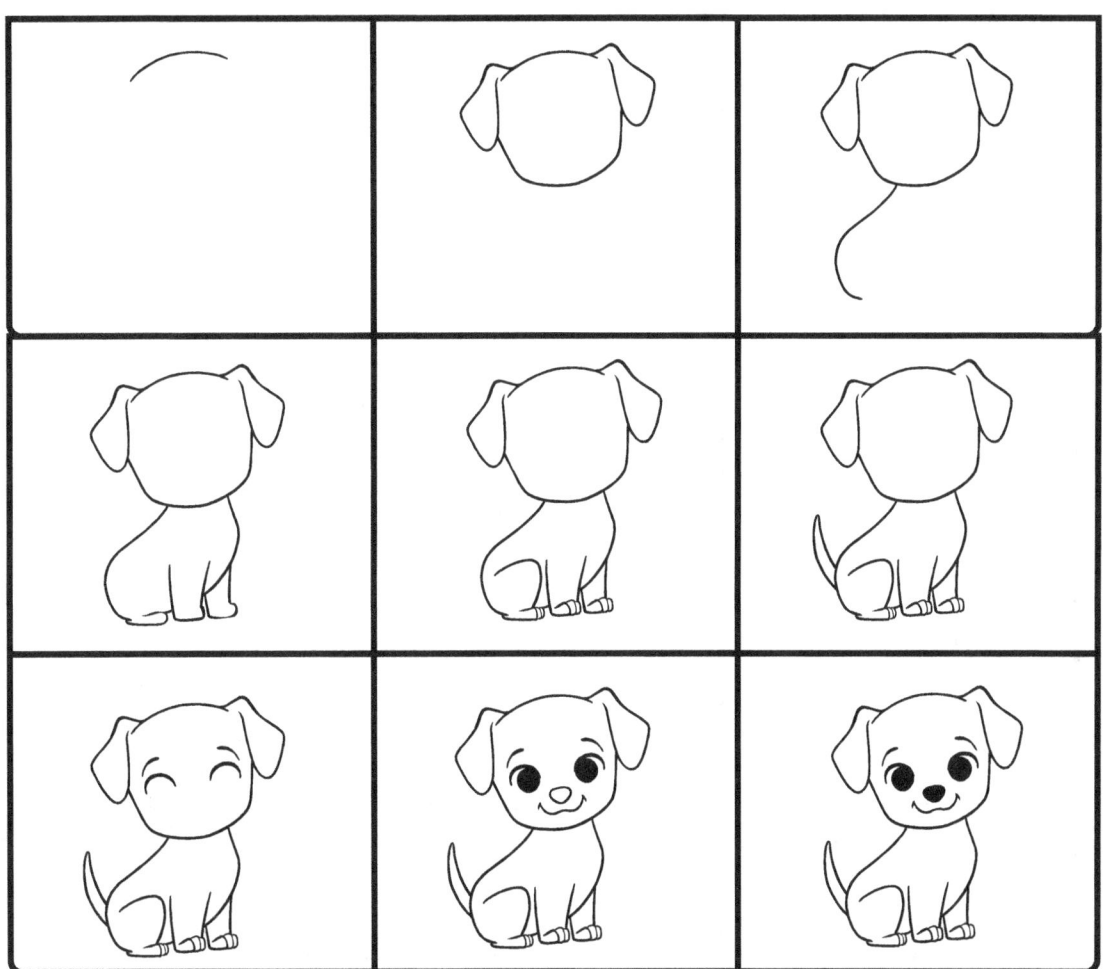

CONNIE

LIVES: LIVES ON A BALCONY IN FRANCE.

LOVES: A BOY CAT ACROSS THE ROAD, BUT SHE'S NEVER ALLOWED OUTSIDE.

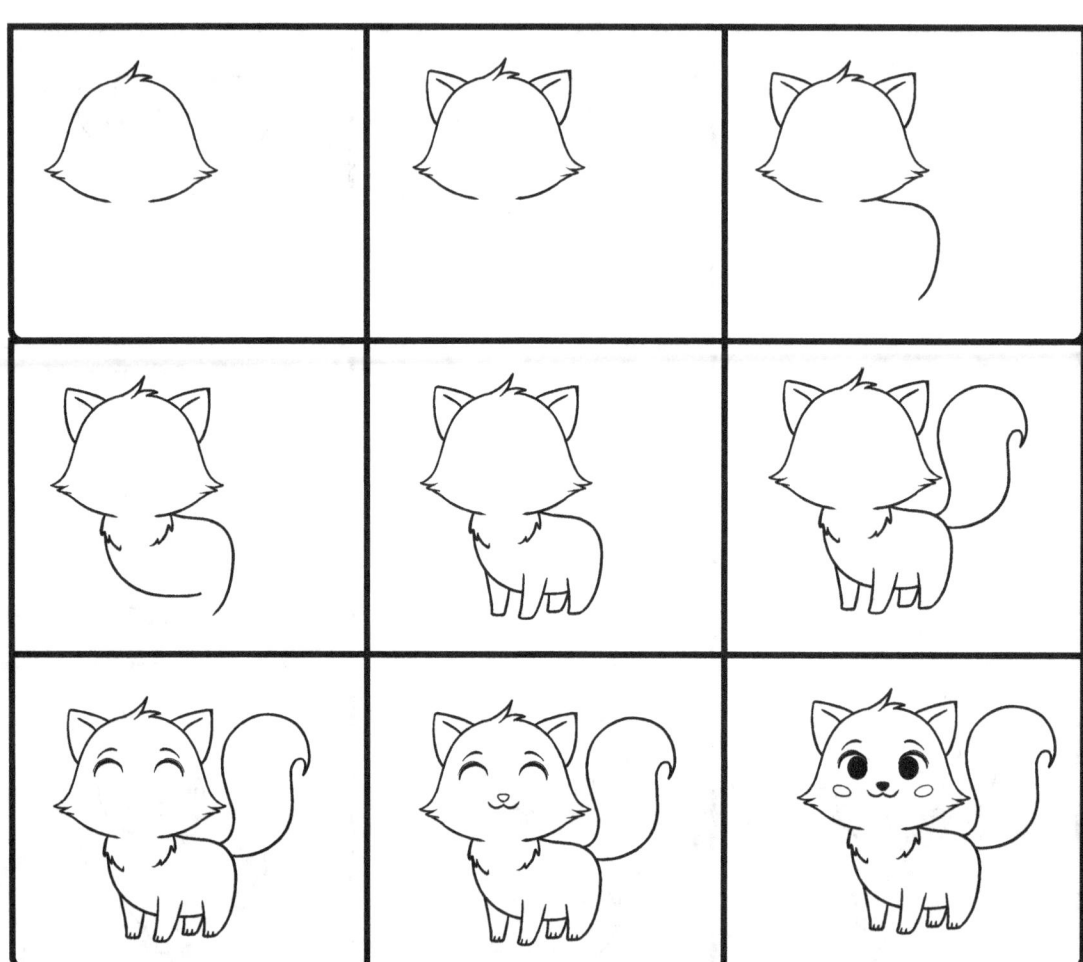

HOW TO DRAW DINOSAURS

CURL-TOP

LIVES: IN AN ICE CREAM SHOP BY THE BEACH.

LOVES: GOING TO THE BEACH, BUT HE MELTS IN A MINUTE!

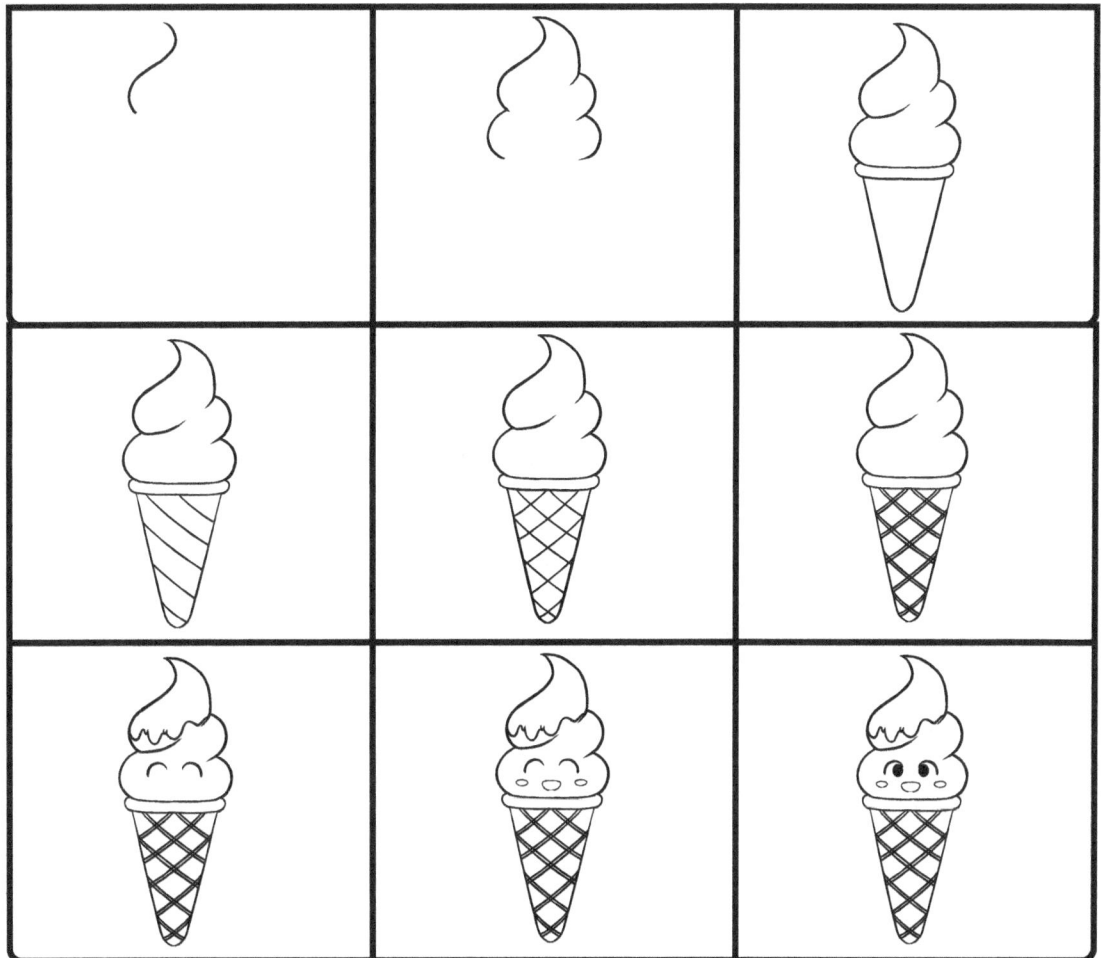

HOW TO DRAW DINOSAURS

CEE-CEE

LIVES: IN A POT IN A CHILD'S YARD.

LOVES: BALLOONS, BUT THEY ALWAYS POP!

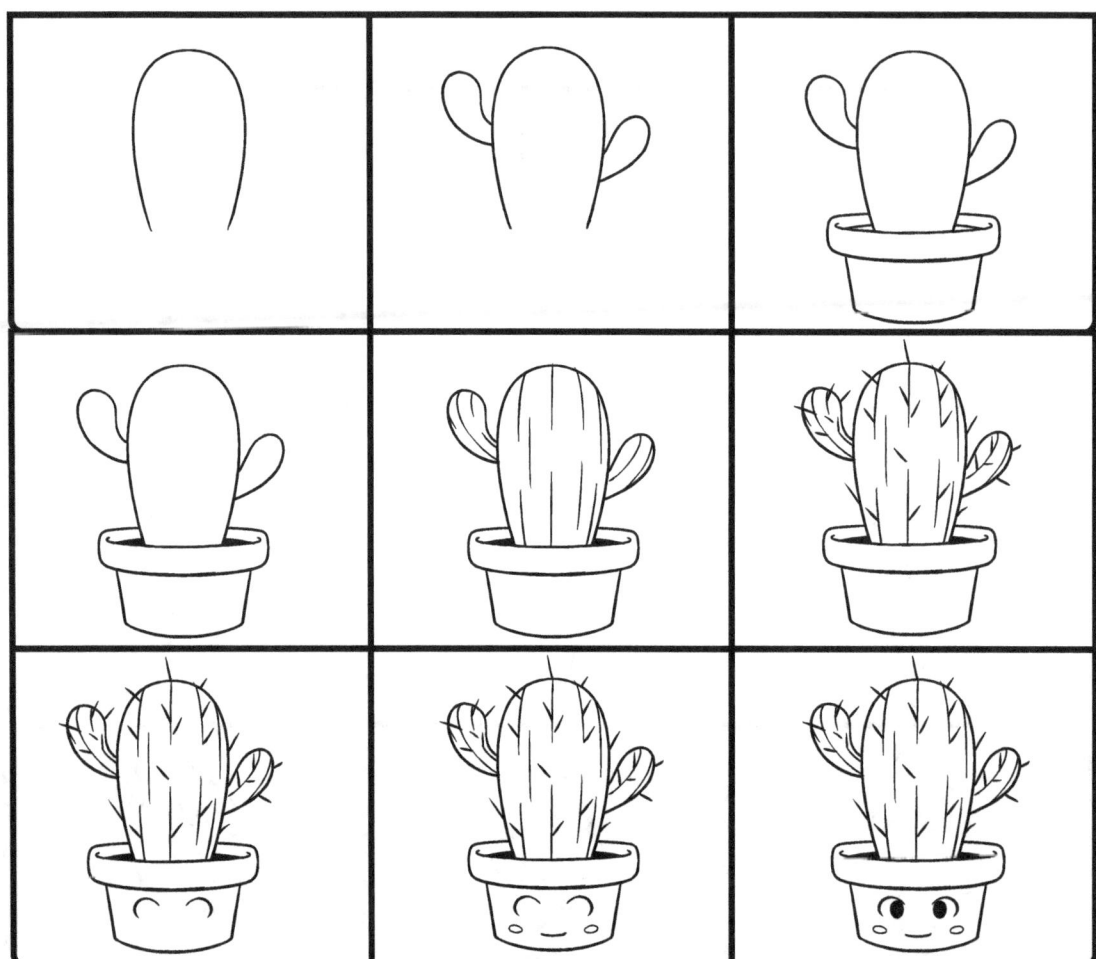

HOW TO DRAW DINOSAURS

SUNSHINE

LIVES: AT A JUICE BAR.

LOVES: BEING MIXED UP WITH OTHER JUICES, BUT NEVER VEGGIES, UGH!

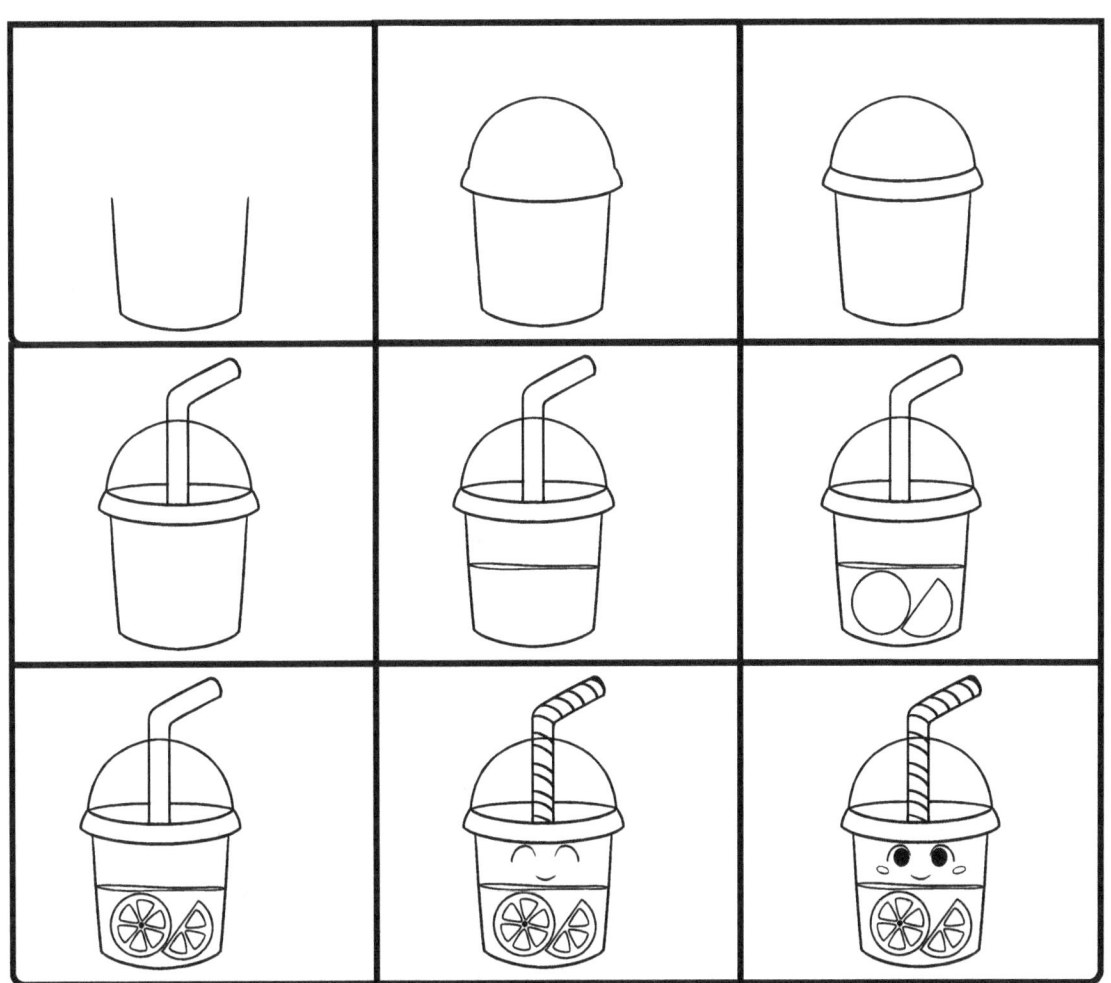

HOW TO DRAW DINOSAURS

SWEETY

LIVES: IN A WARREN NOT FAR FROM A LOVELY SANDY BEACH.

LOVES: HOW SOFT HER FLUFFY TAIL IS, AND HOPPING AS HIGH AS SHE CAN.

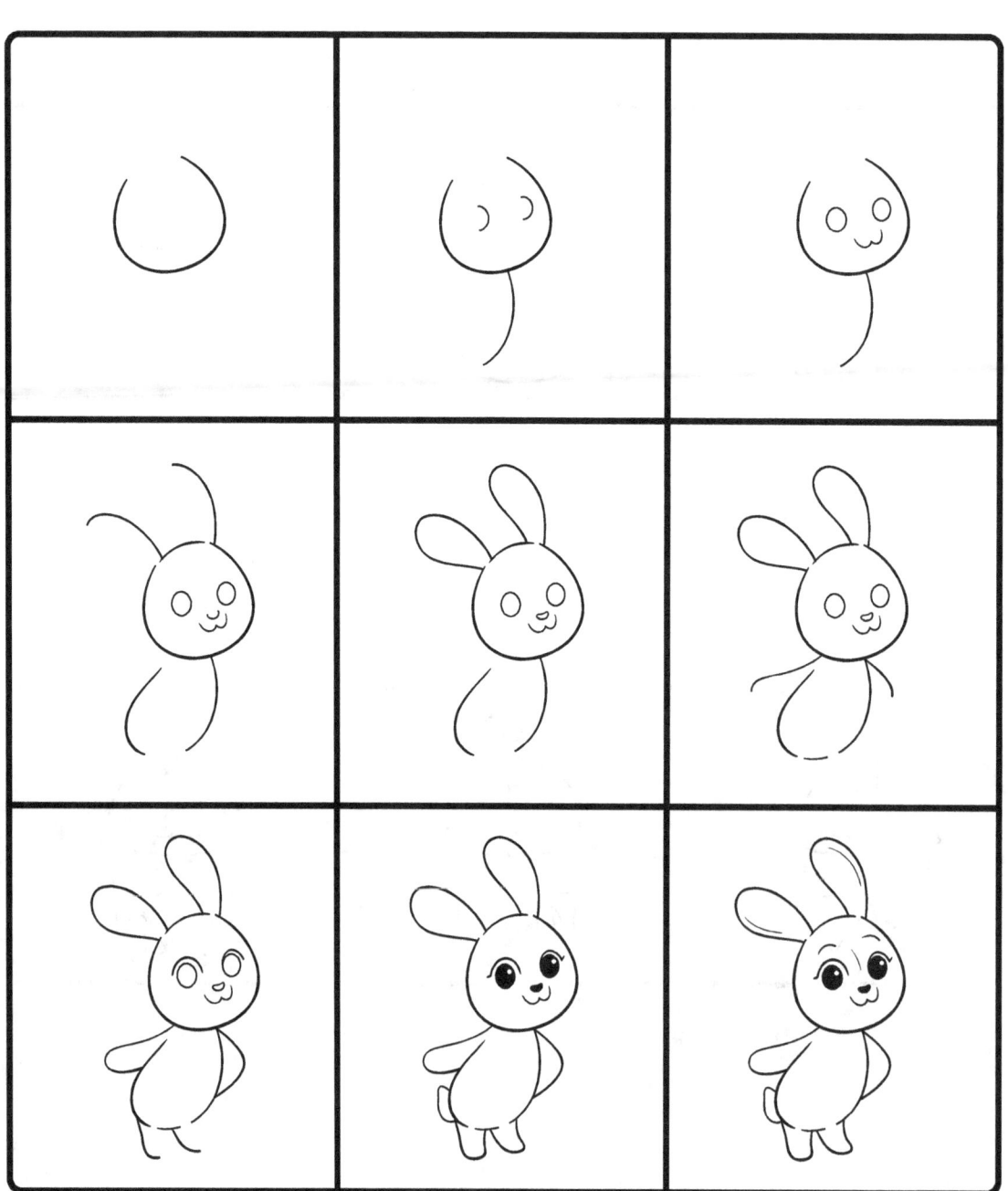

HOW TO DRAW DINOSAURS

TIGS

LIVES: IN LONG TALL GRASS.

LOVES: PLAYING HIDE AND SEEK, BUT NO ONE EVER FINDS HIM, EVER.

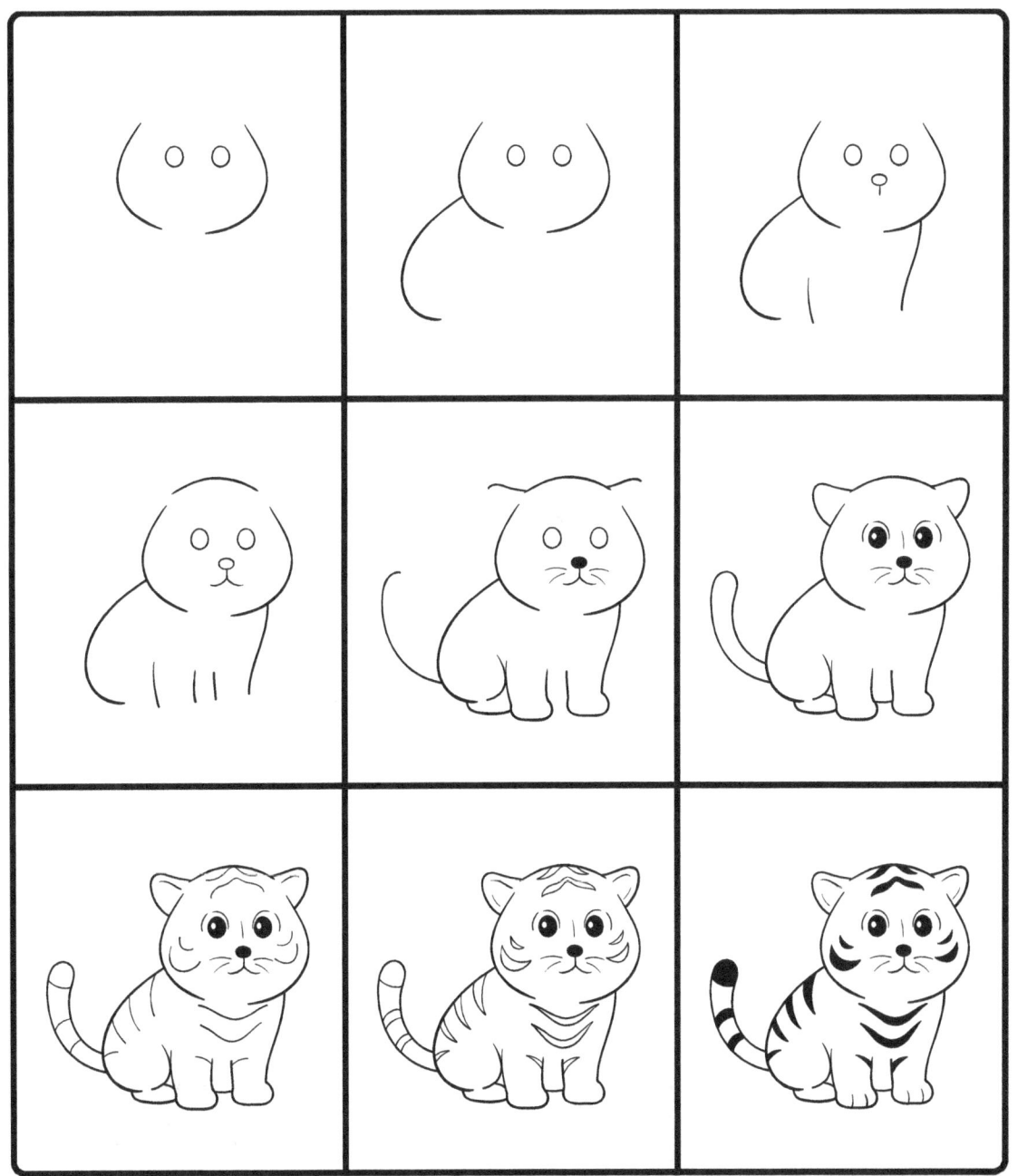

HOW TO DRAW DINOSAURS

ANTIPODES

LIVES: IN A ZOO IN ENGLAND.

LOVES: ELEPHANTS, BUT THEIR HUGS ARE TOO TIGHT!

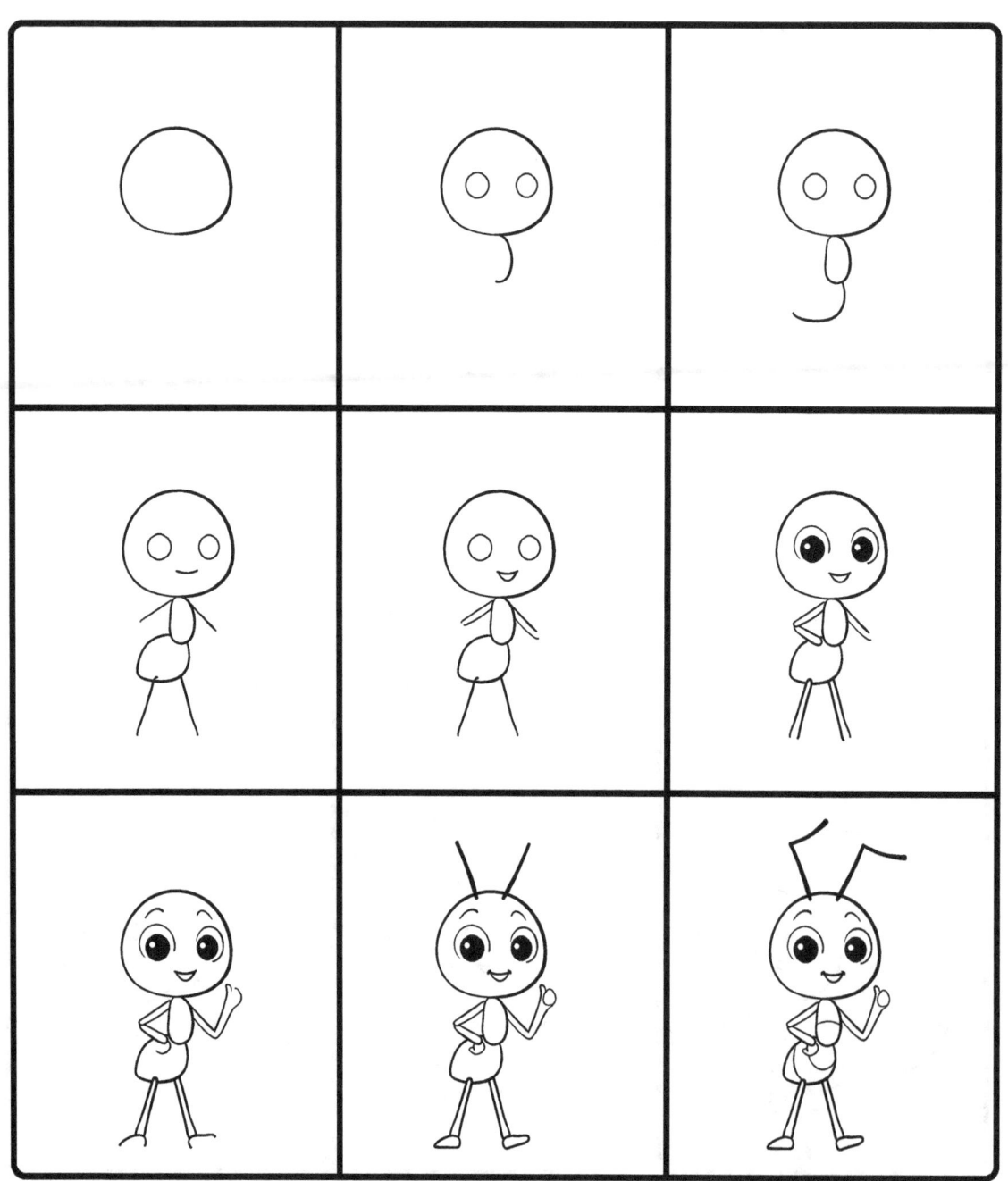

HOW TO DRAW DINOSAURS
15

SNIG

LIVES: IN A MUDDY PIGSTY.

LOVES: CHOCOLATE. IT LOOKS A LOT LIKE MUD, BUT THAT TASTE; UGH!

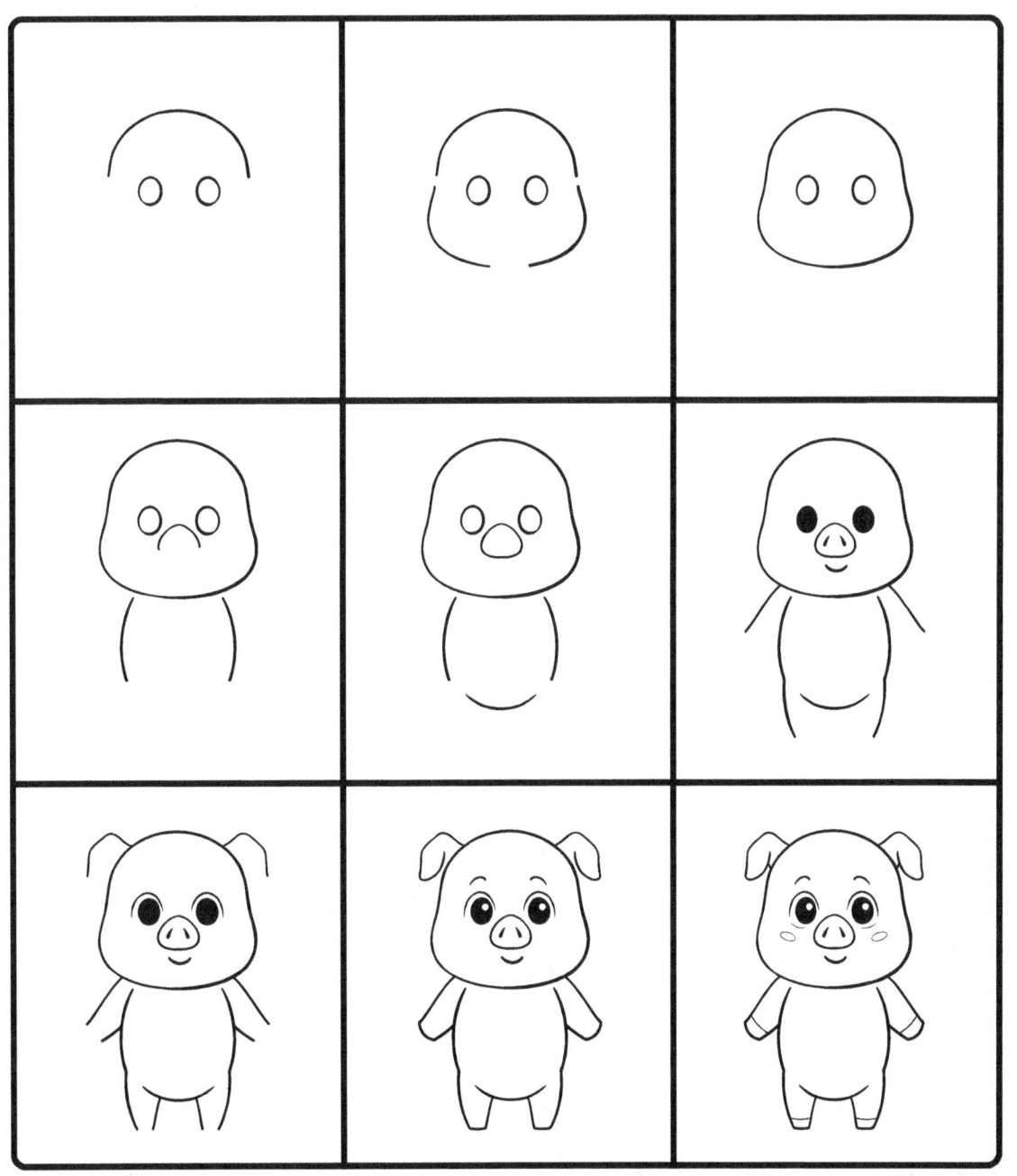

HOW TO DRAW DINOSAURS

SPEEDY

LIVES: IN A COTTAGE GARDEN.

LOVES: LOVES RACING COMPETITIONS, BUT ALWAYS COMES LAST.

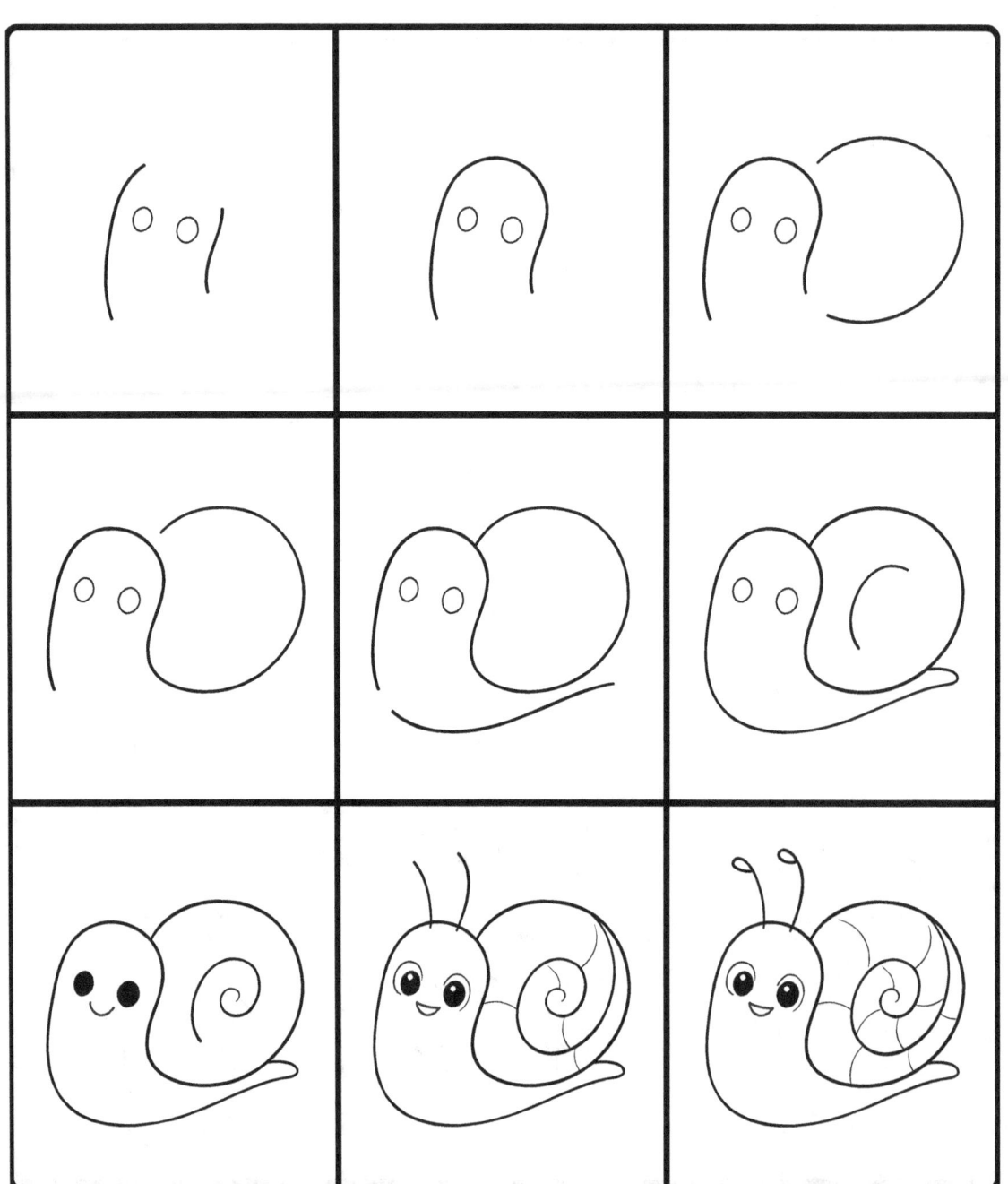

RATTUS

LIVES: IN A HOLE IN THE WALL OF A FANCY HOUSE.

LOVES: PLAYING DRESS UPS TO SCARE THE CAT!

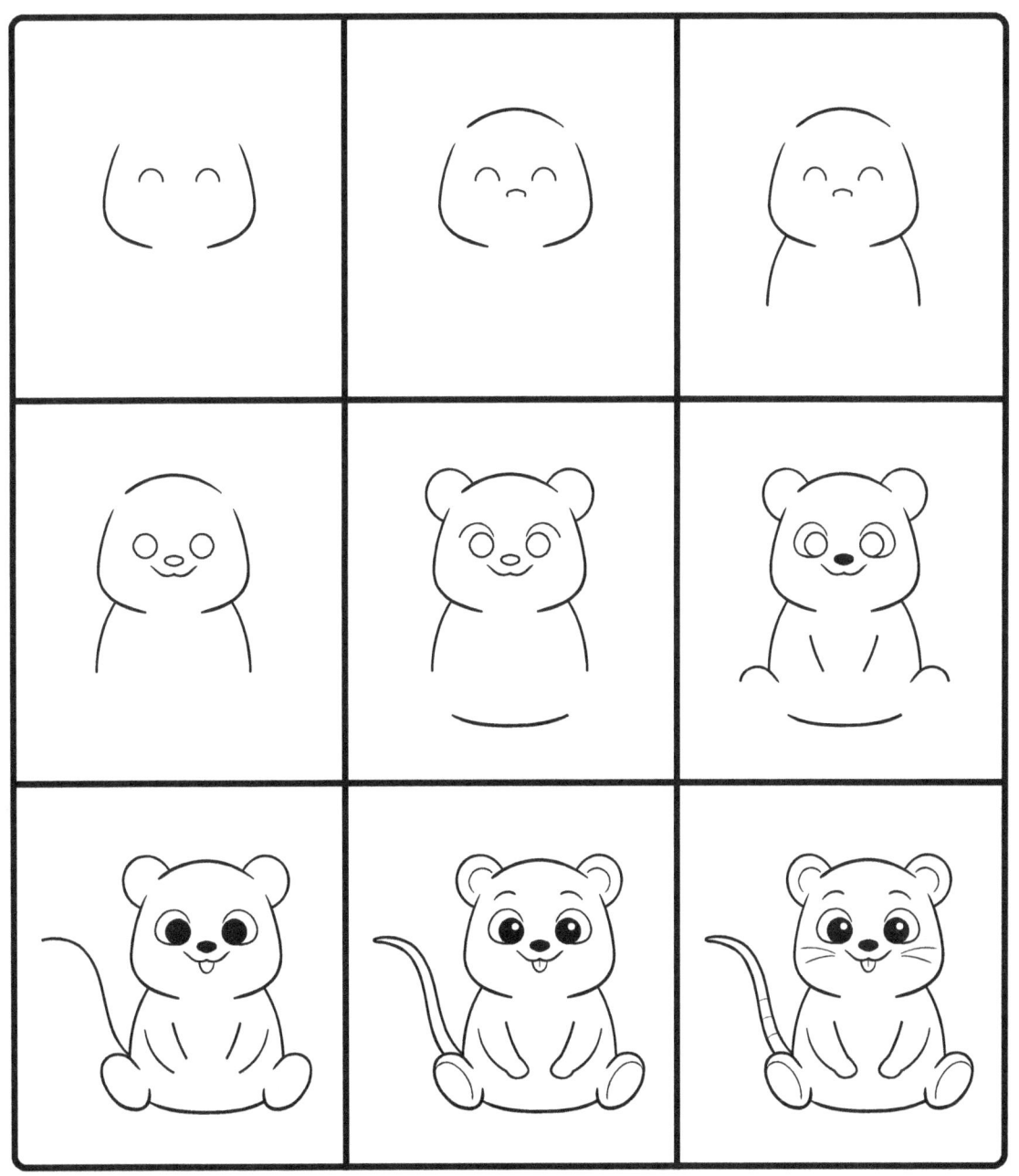

SQUISH

LIVES: ON THE OUTSKIRTS OF A COUNTRY TOWN.

LOVES: TO BE CUDDLED AND TOLD, 'OH YOU'RE SO CUTE!' BUT THE TEDDY BEARS GET ALL THE ATTENTION.

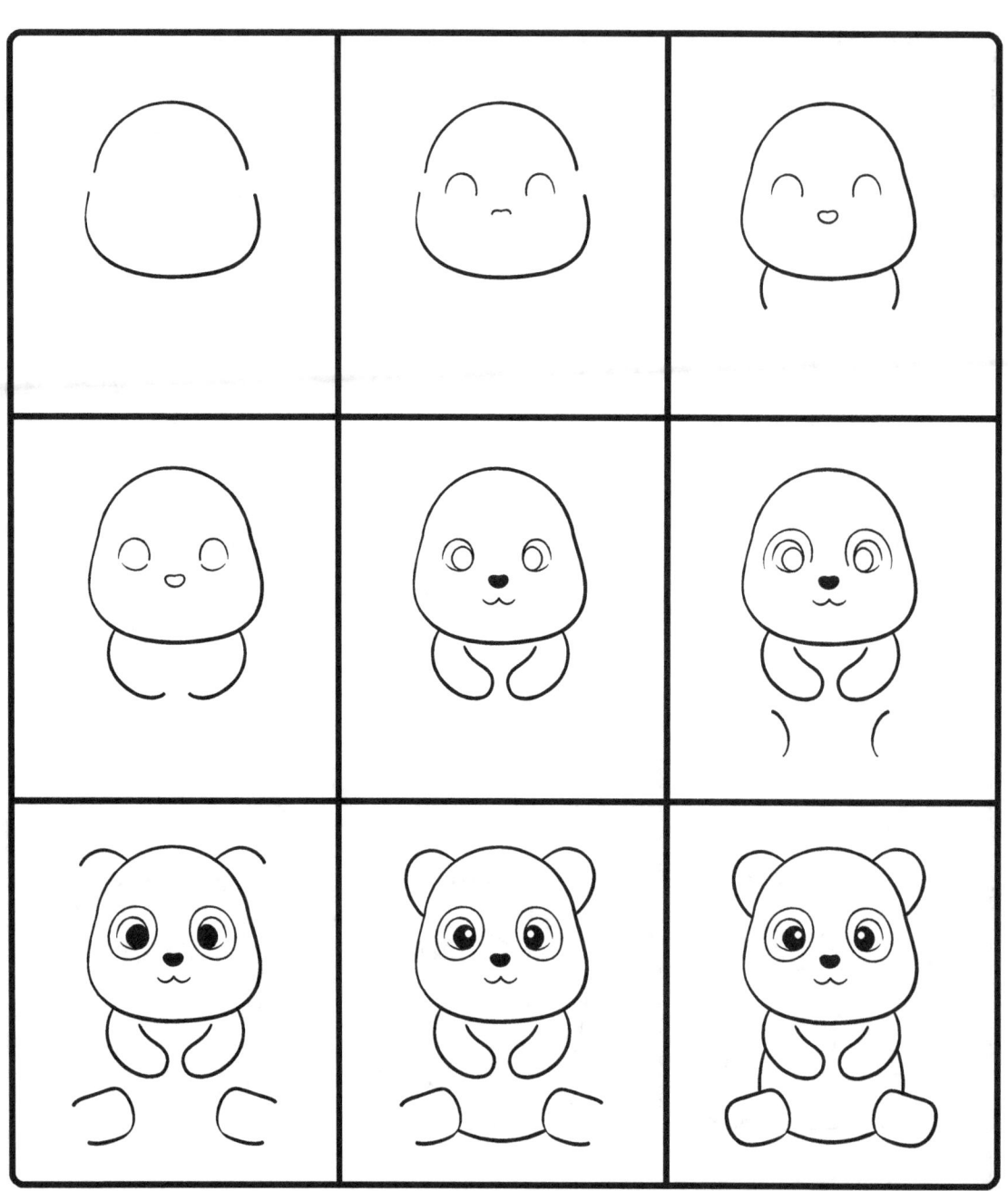

HOW TO DRAW DINOSAURS

DOTTY

LIVES: BESIDE A POPULAR HIKING TRAIL.

LOVES: TO GIVE AND GET HUGS, BUT KIDS ARE A LITTLE SCARED.

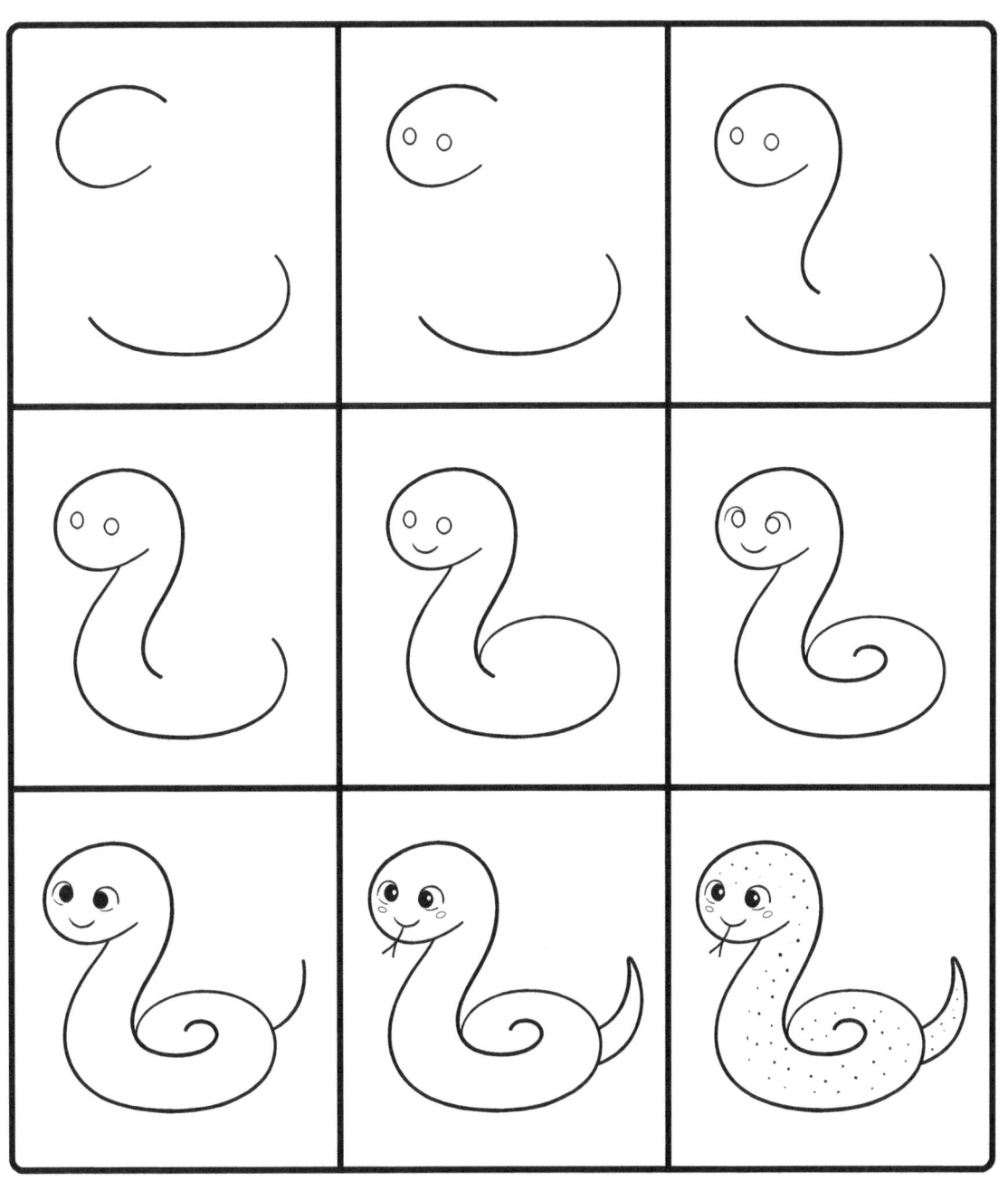

MONKEM

LIVES: IN BALI, AT A POPULAR TEMPLE.

LOVES: SWIPING THINGS FROM TOURISTS.

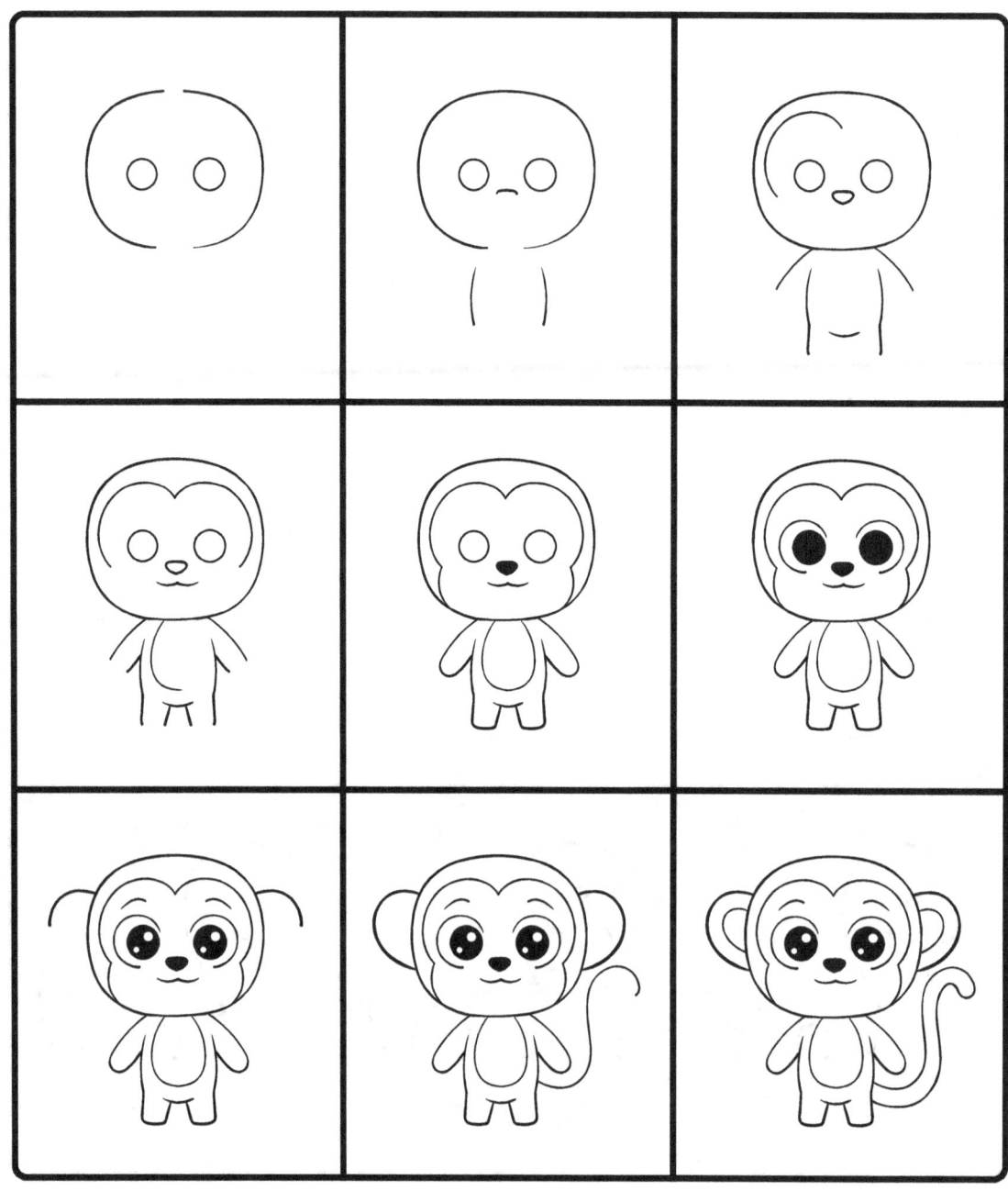

HOW TO DRAW DINOSAURS

MOOGIE

LIVES: ON A FARM IN THE AUSTRALIAN COUNTRYSIDE.

LOVES: PLAYING WITH THE SHEEPDOGS.

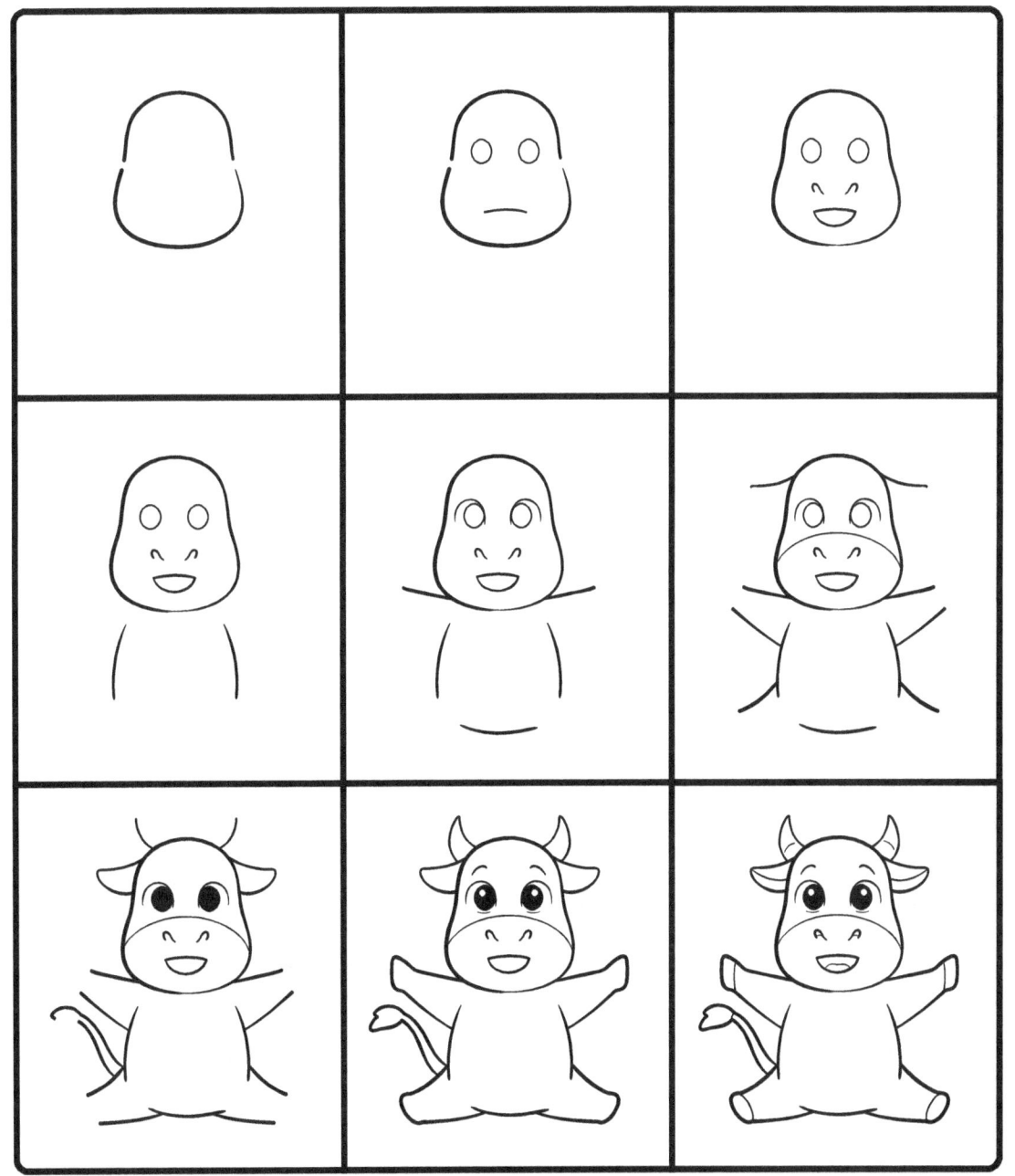

HOW TO DRAW DINOSAURS

FINNSTER

LIVES: IN A FISH TANK IN A FANCY HOTEL.

LOVES: TO WRITE STORIES, AND THE PAPER ALWAYS GETS WET!

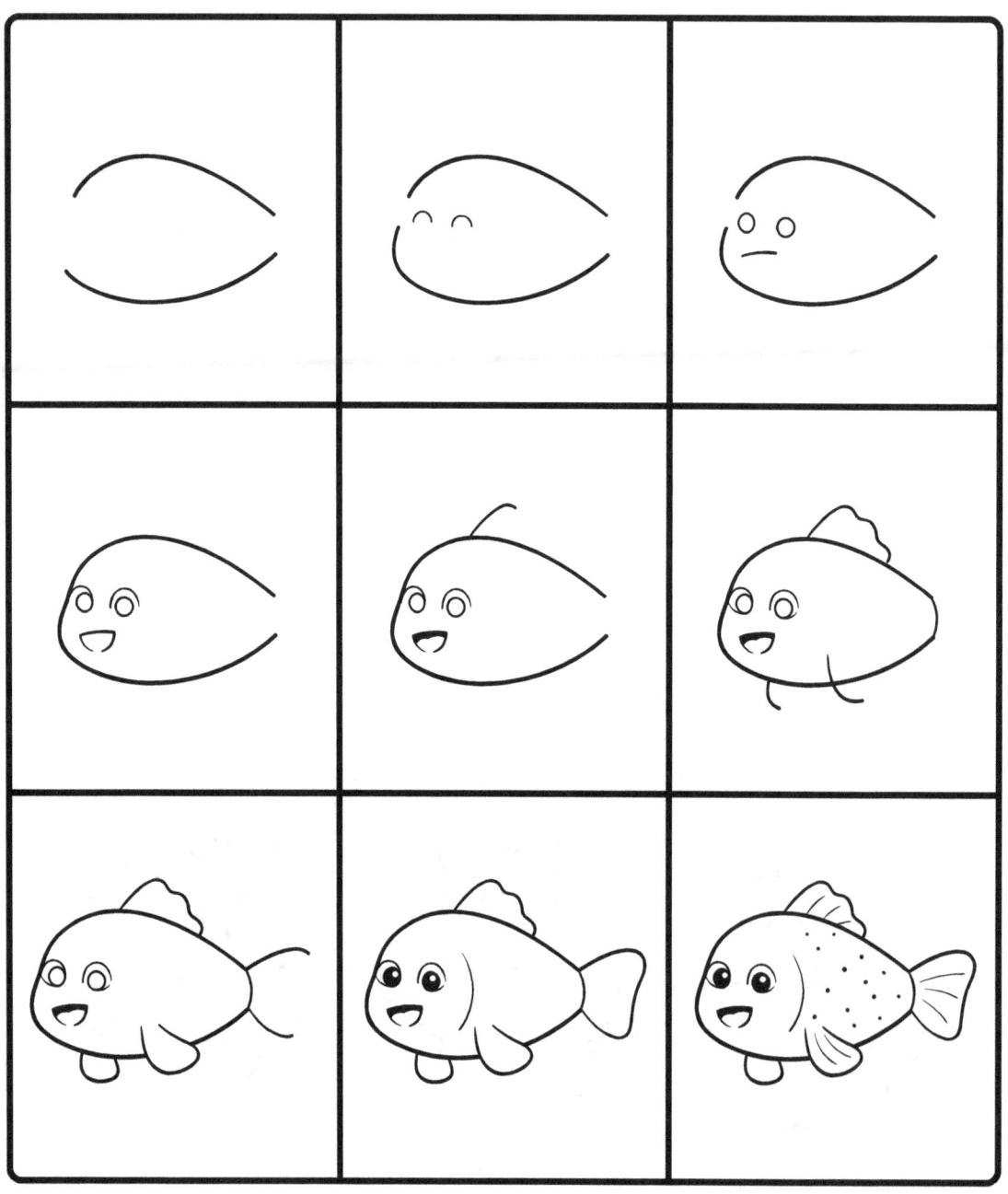

HOW TO DRAW DINOSAURS
23

FLAP

LIVES: AT THE TOP OF A TALL, TALL TREE.

LOVES: TO FLY WITH THE SUN ON ITS WINGS, BUT IS ALWAYS ASLEEP IN THE DAY.

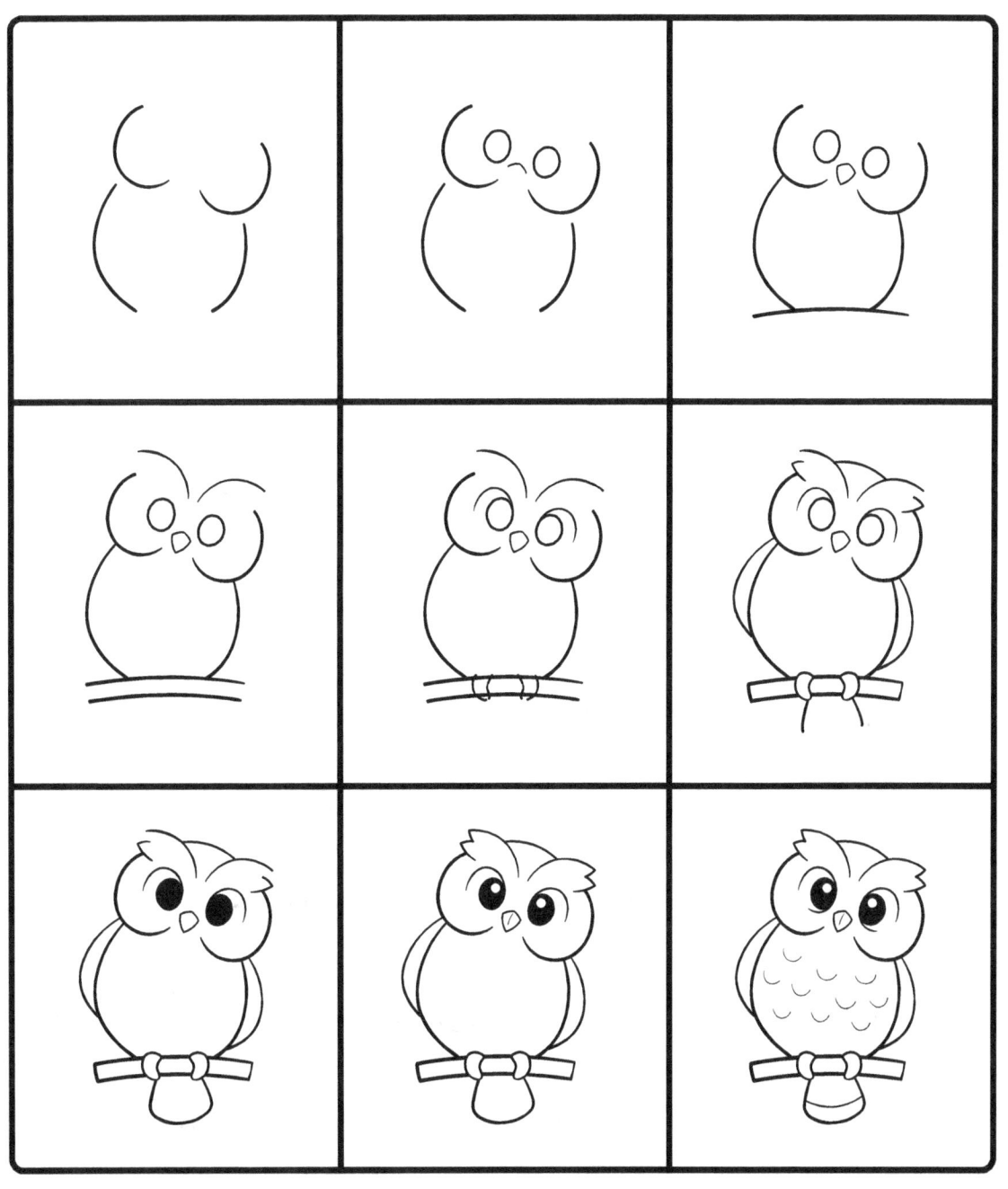

SAURY

LIVES: ONLY IN BOOKS!

LOVES: HAVING HIS SKELETON ON SHOW IN MUSEUMS AROUND THE WORLD.

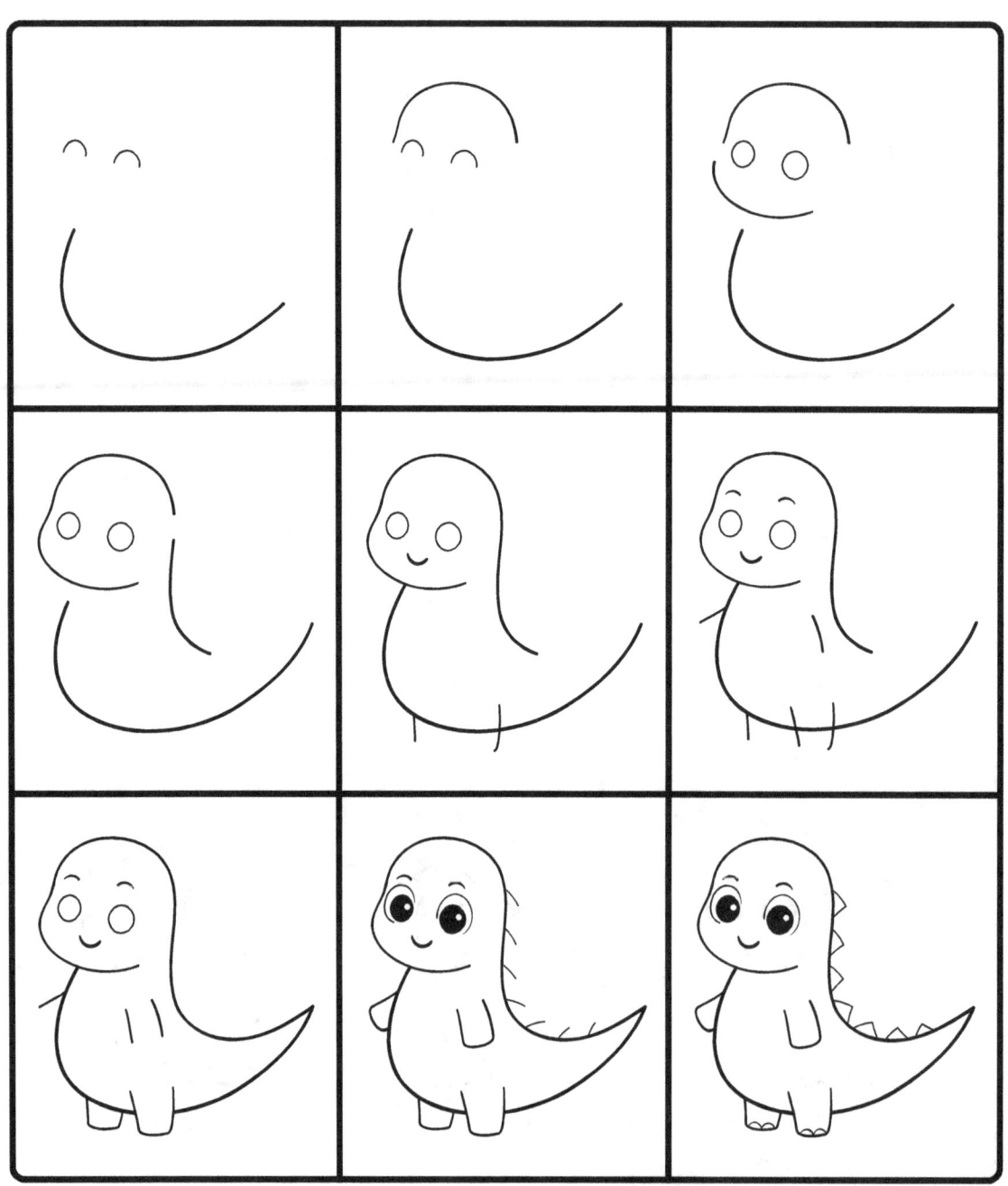

HOW TO DRAW DINOSAURS

FLIT

LIVES: ON THE EDGES OF A MAPLE FOREST.

LOVES: AUTUMN, AND FLYING THROUGH THE MAGICAL CHANGING COLORS OF THE LEAVES.

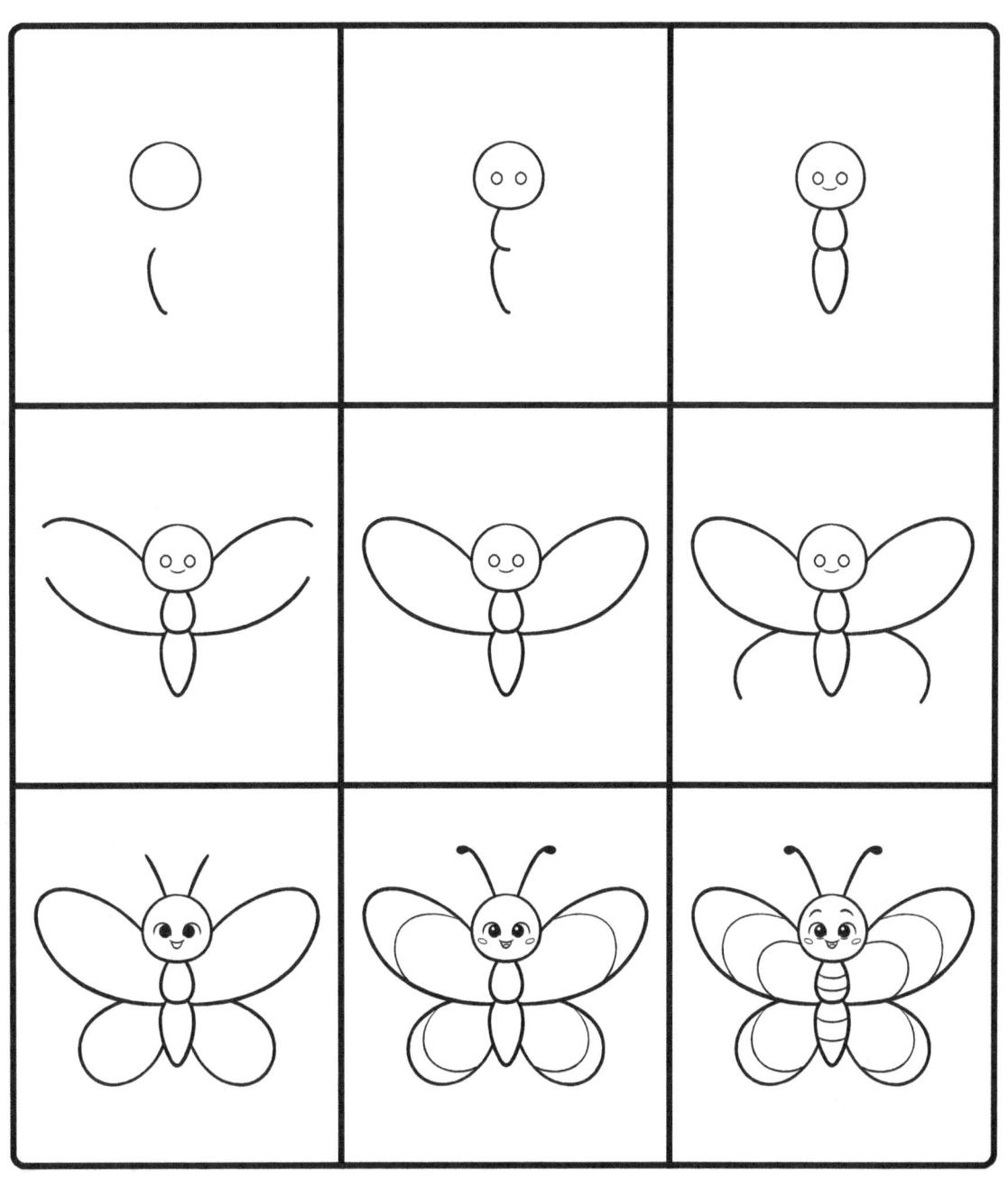

HOW TO DRAW DINOSAURS

SCAT

LIVES: WITH HIS SISTER, SKIP.

LOVES: TO PLAY WITH HIS SISTER, SKIP, BUT HE'S SICK OF DRESS-UPS AND BRACELET-MAKING.

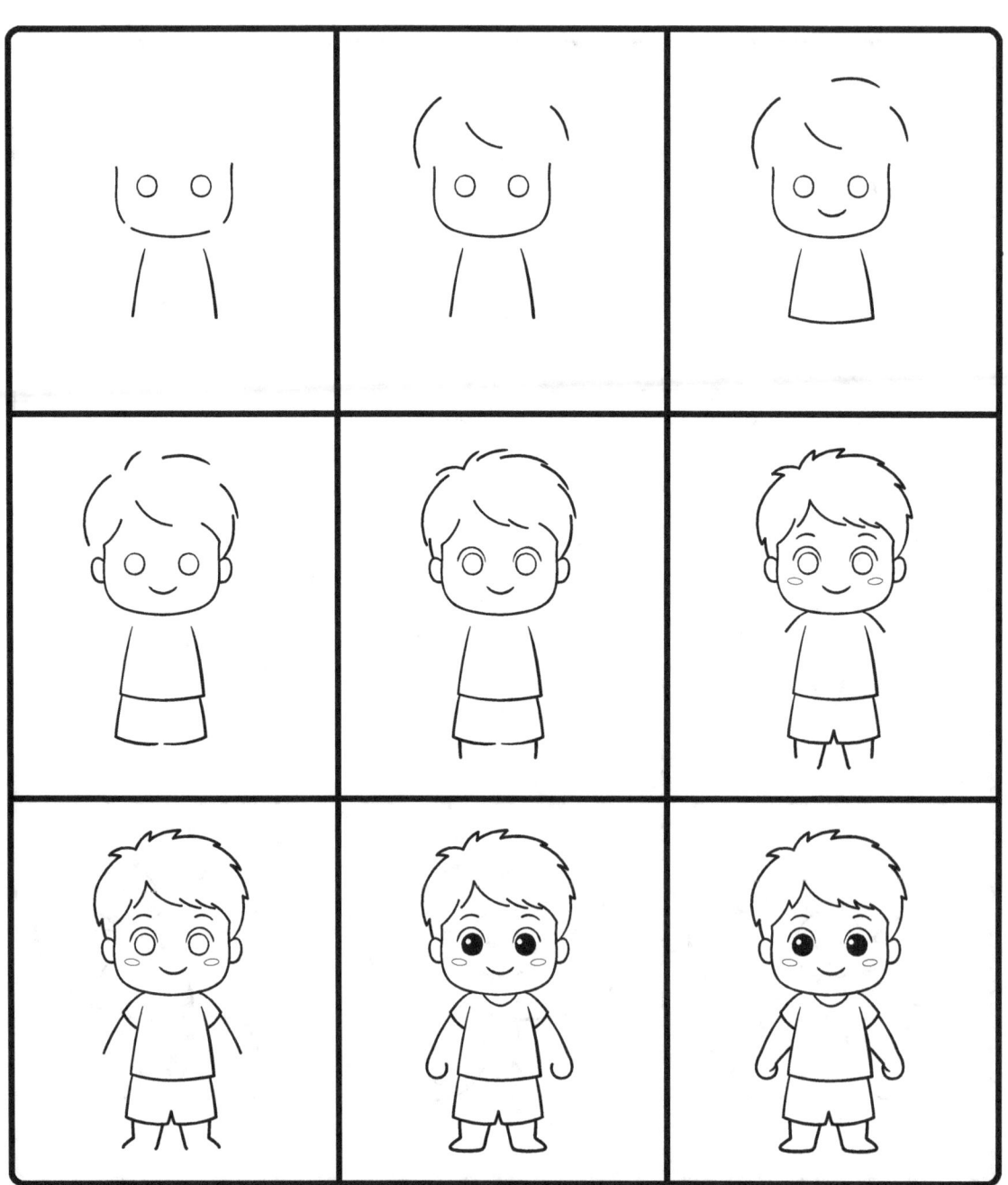

HOW TO DRAW DINOSAURS

SKIP

LIVES: WITH HER BROTHER, SCAT.

LOVES: TO PLAY WITH HER BROTHER, SCAT, BUT SHE'S SICK OF SWORD FIGHTS AND BUG CATCHING.

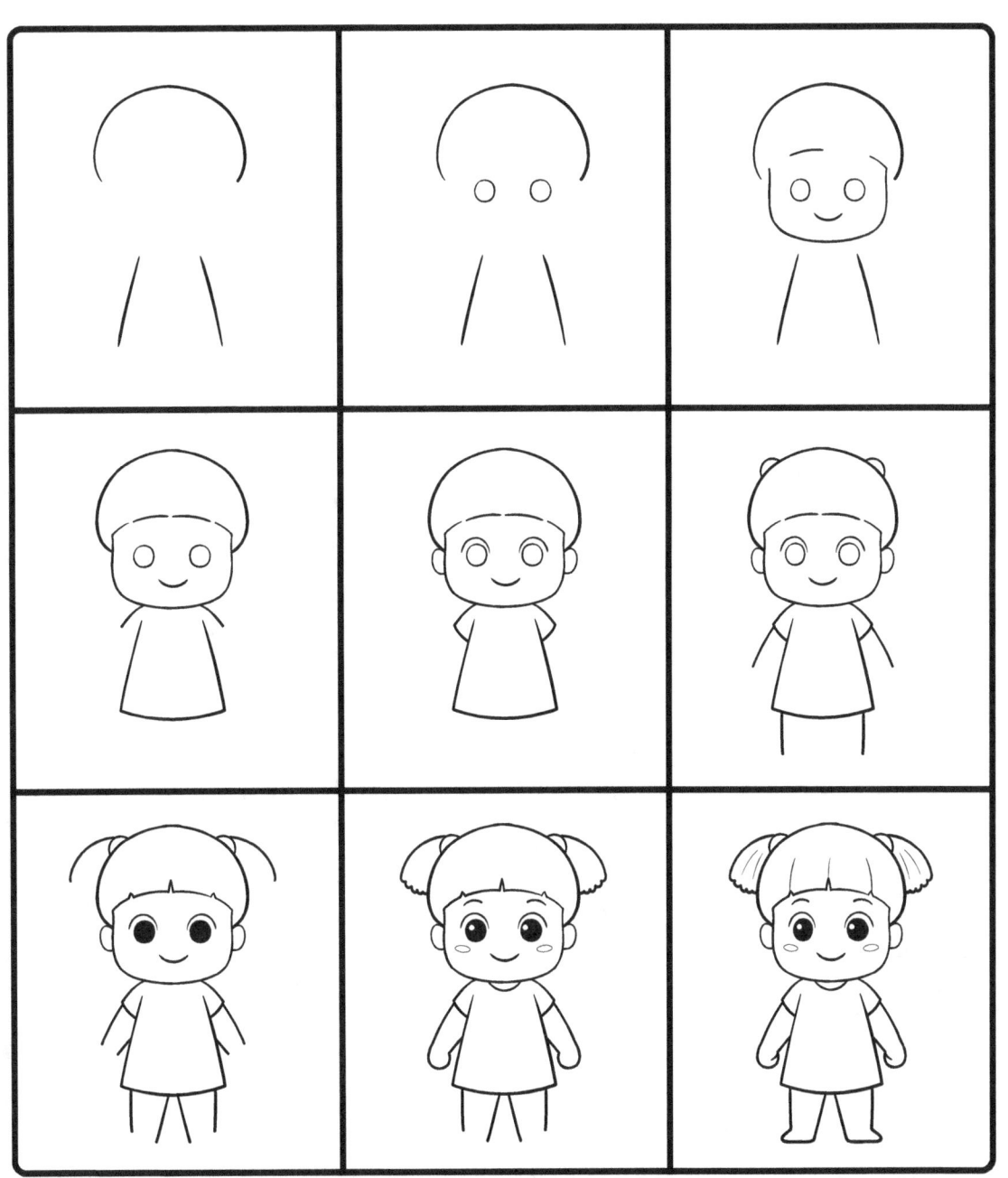

HOW TO DRAW DINOSAURS

DOLLY

LIVES: IN DOLPHIN COVE WHERE LOTS OF TOURISTS COME TO PAT HER.

LOVES: LOVES A PAT, BUT LOVES EVEN MORE THAT SHE IS FREE TO COME AND GO AS SHE PLEASES.

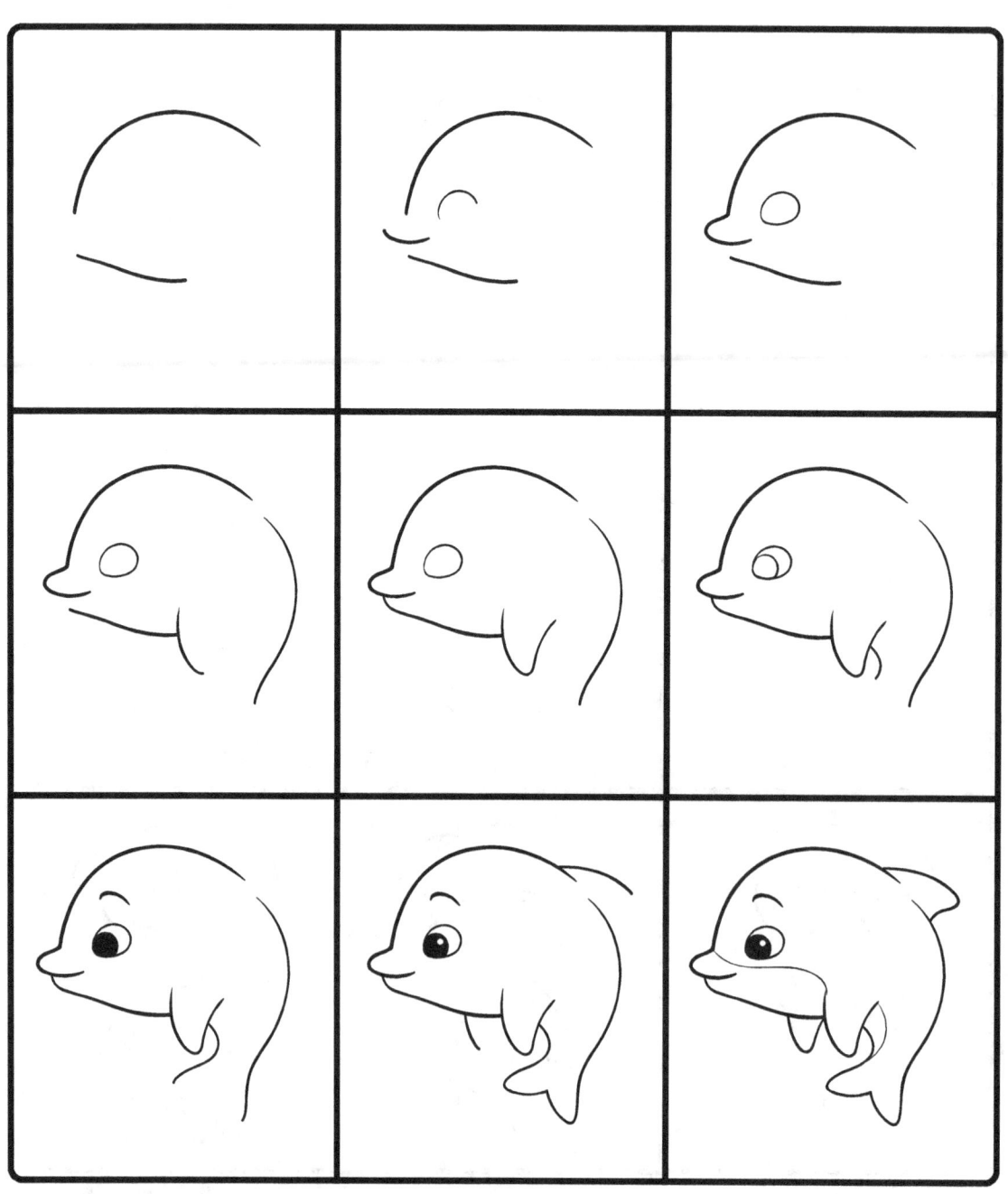

SNUGS

LIVES: IN A COFFEE SHOP.

LOVES: PUTTING SMILES ON PEOPLE'S FACES AS THEY TAKE THEIR FIRST SIP.

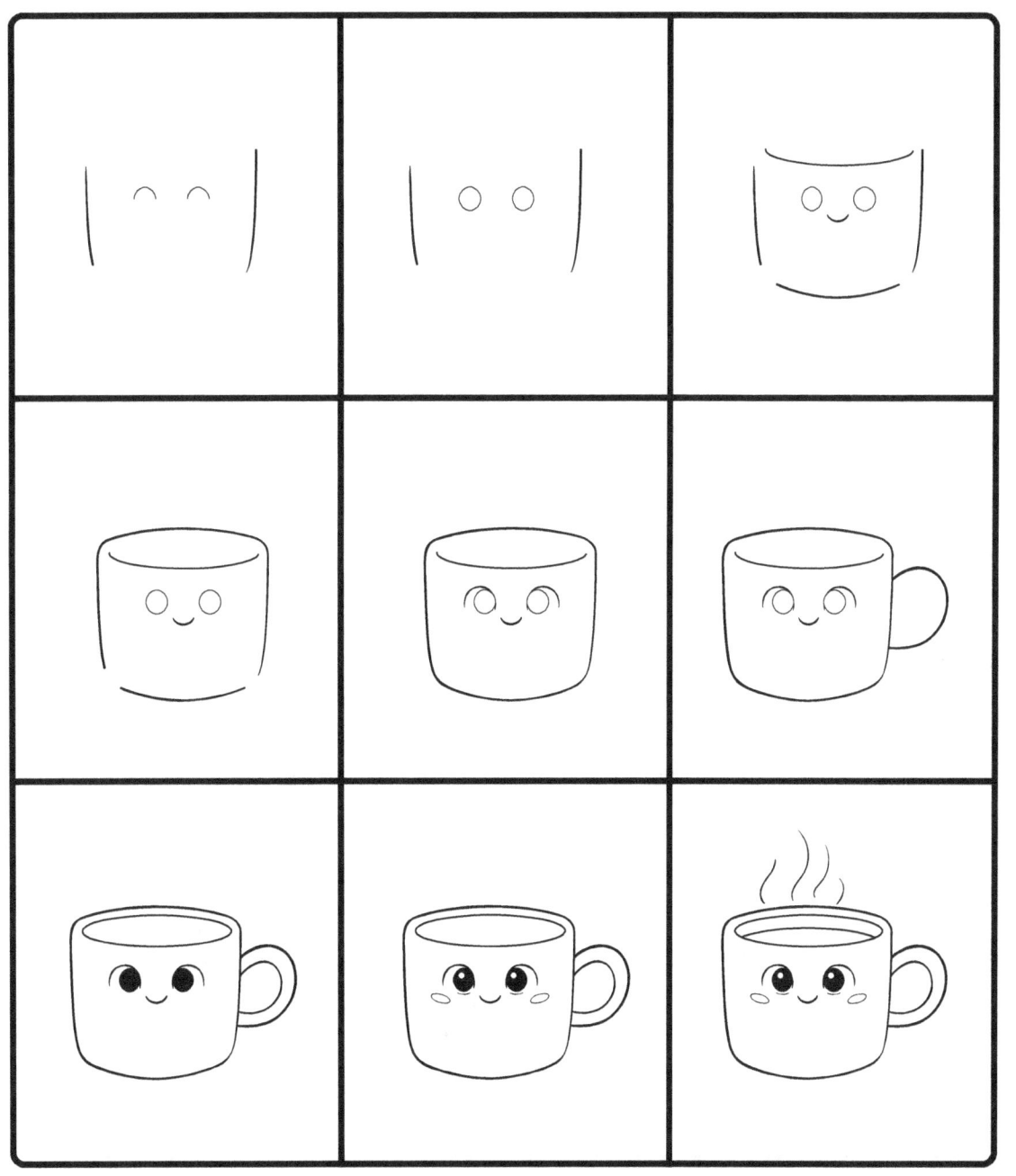

HOW TO DRAW DINOSAURS

BEAKY

LIVES: IN A PINE FOREST.

LOVES: WORMS, BUT HATES HAVING TO GET UP SO EARLY!

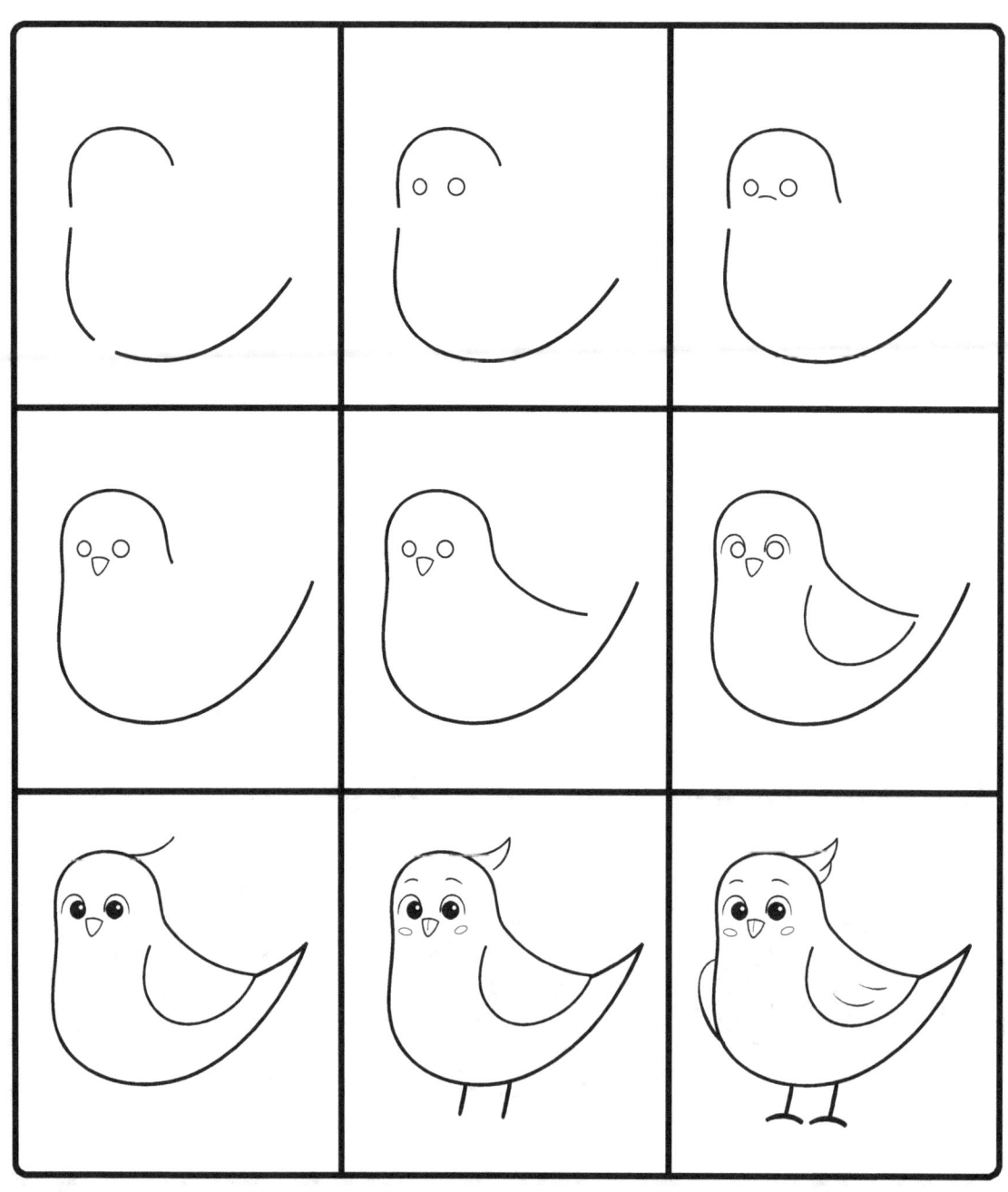

HOW TO DRAW DINOSAURS

31

GIRLY

LIVES: ON A FARM OWNED BY A LOVELY FAMILY.

LOVES: WAKING UP JUST AS THE SUN STARTS TO SHINE, THEN WAKING EVERYONE ELSE UP!

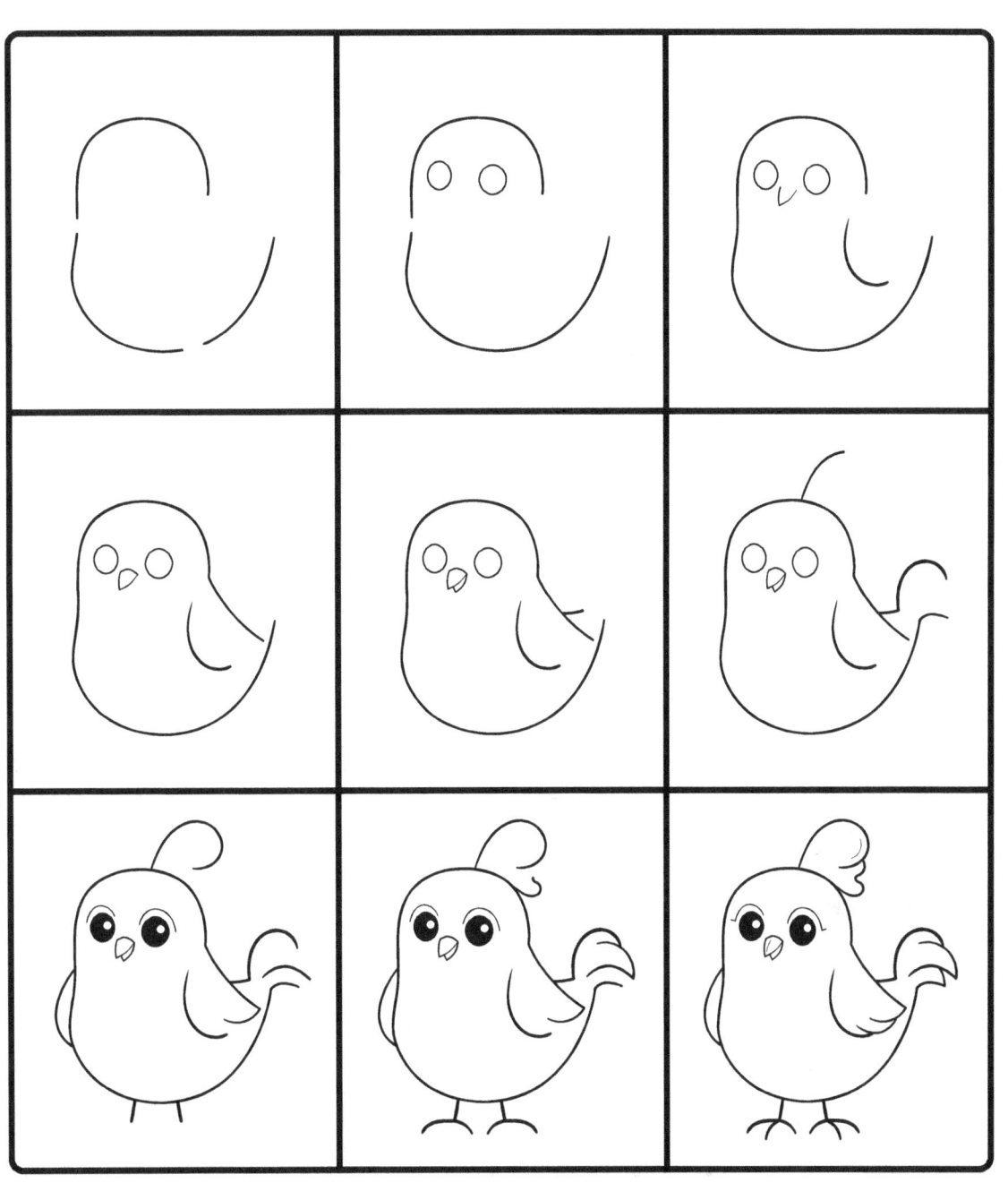

HOW TO DRAW DINOSAURS

SHELBY

LIVES: JUST OFF THE COAST OF MIAMI.

LOVES: TO BREAKDANCE BUT GETS STUCK ON HIS BACK.

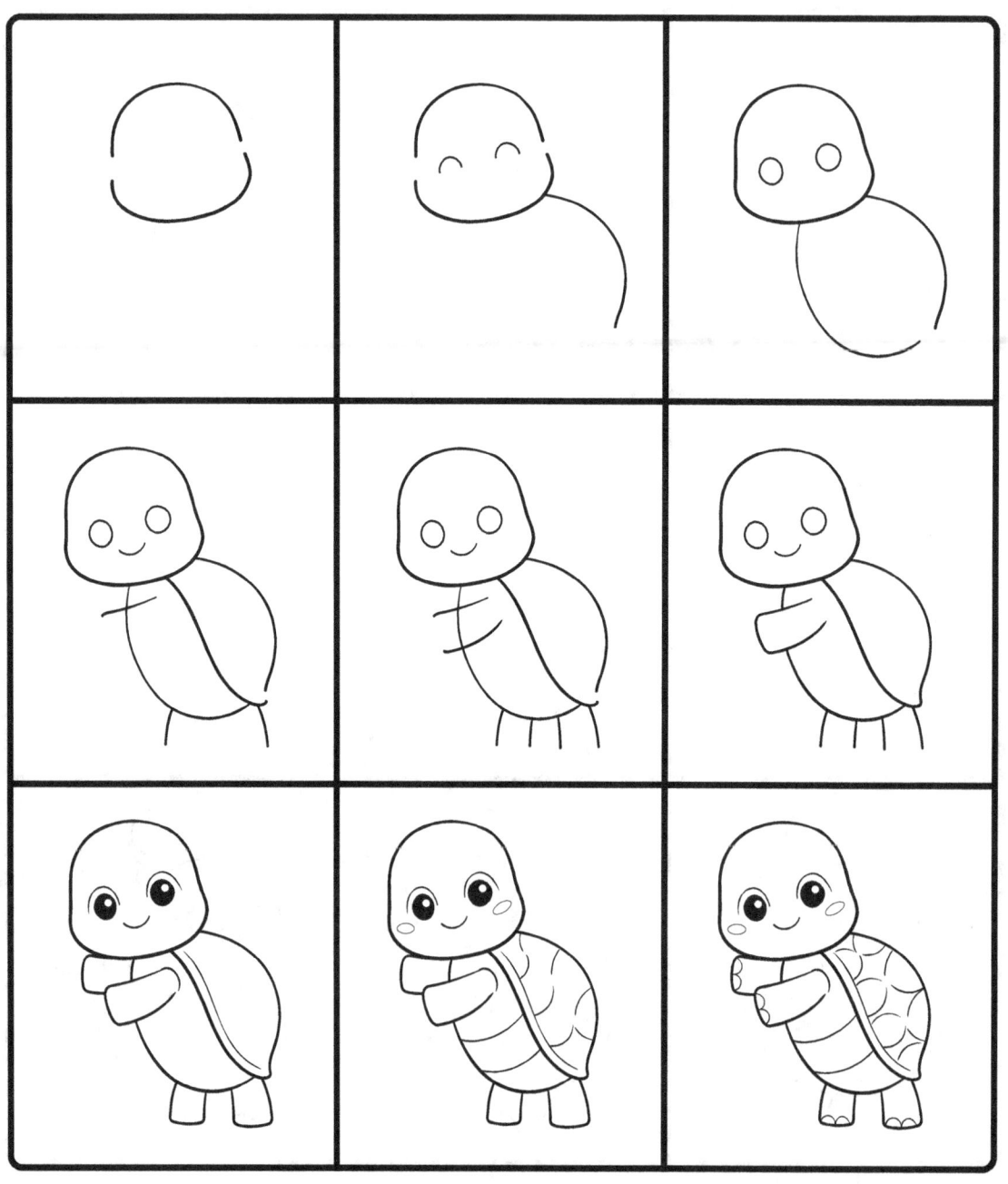

HOW TO DRAW DINOSAURS

33

DRIFTER

LIVES: IN A FRONT YARD, IN FRONT OF THE WINDOW OF A HOME.

LOVES: A COZY FIREPLACE IN WINTER, WITH A GOOD BOOK... CAN'T STAY FOR LONG THOUGH!

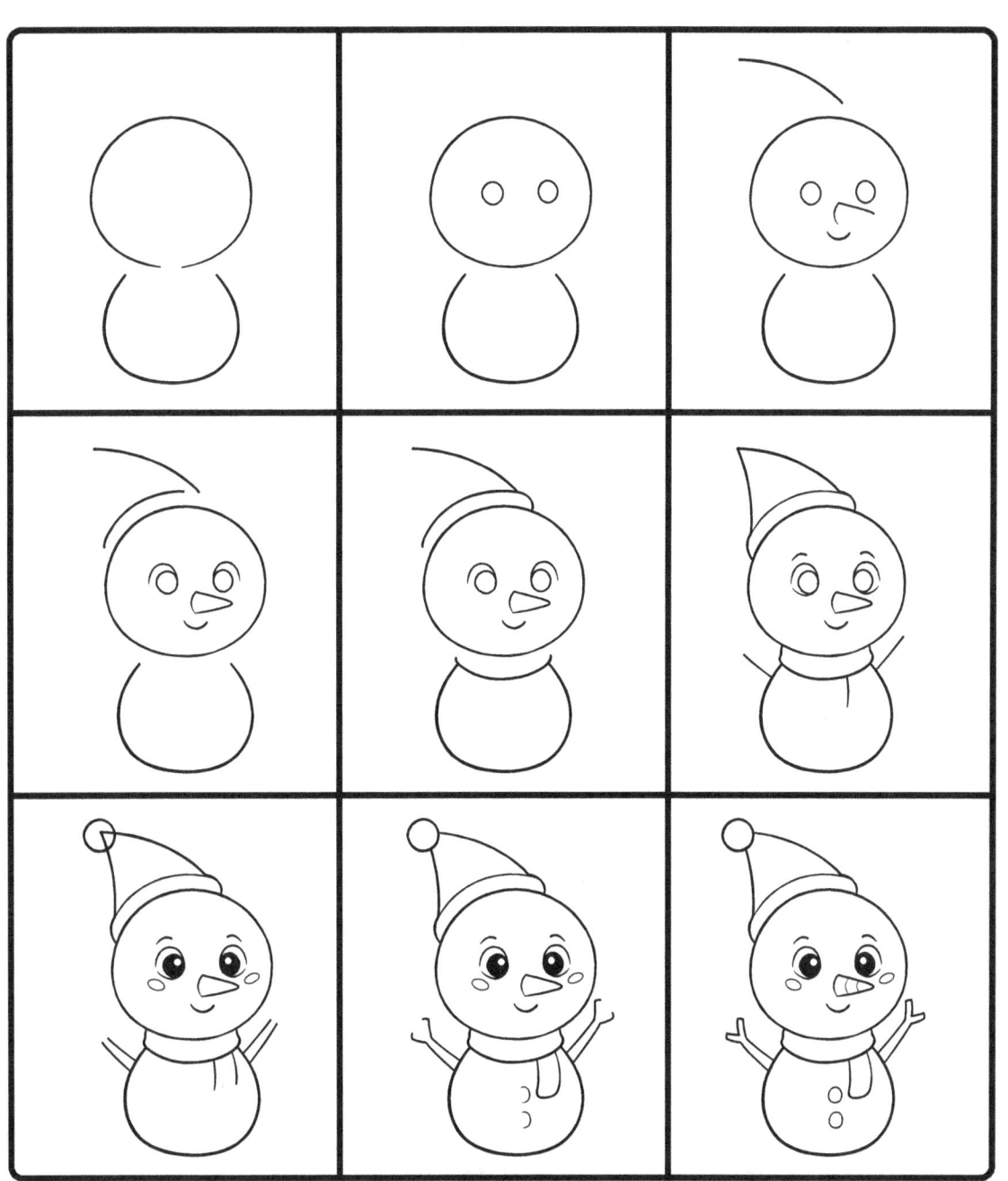

HOW TO DRAW DINOSAURS

ROB

LIVES: AT HOME AS A SERVANT AND COOK.

LOVES: BEING SO CLEVER BUT WOULD LOVE TO KNOW WHAT IT'S LIKE TO BE ALIVE!

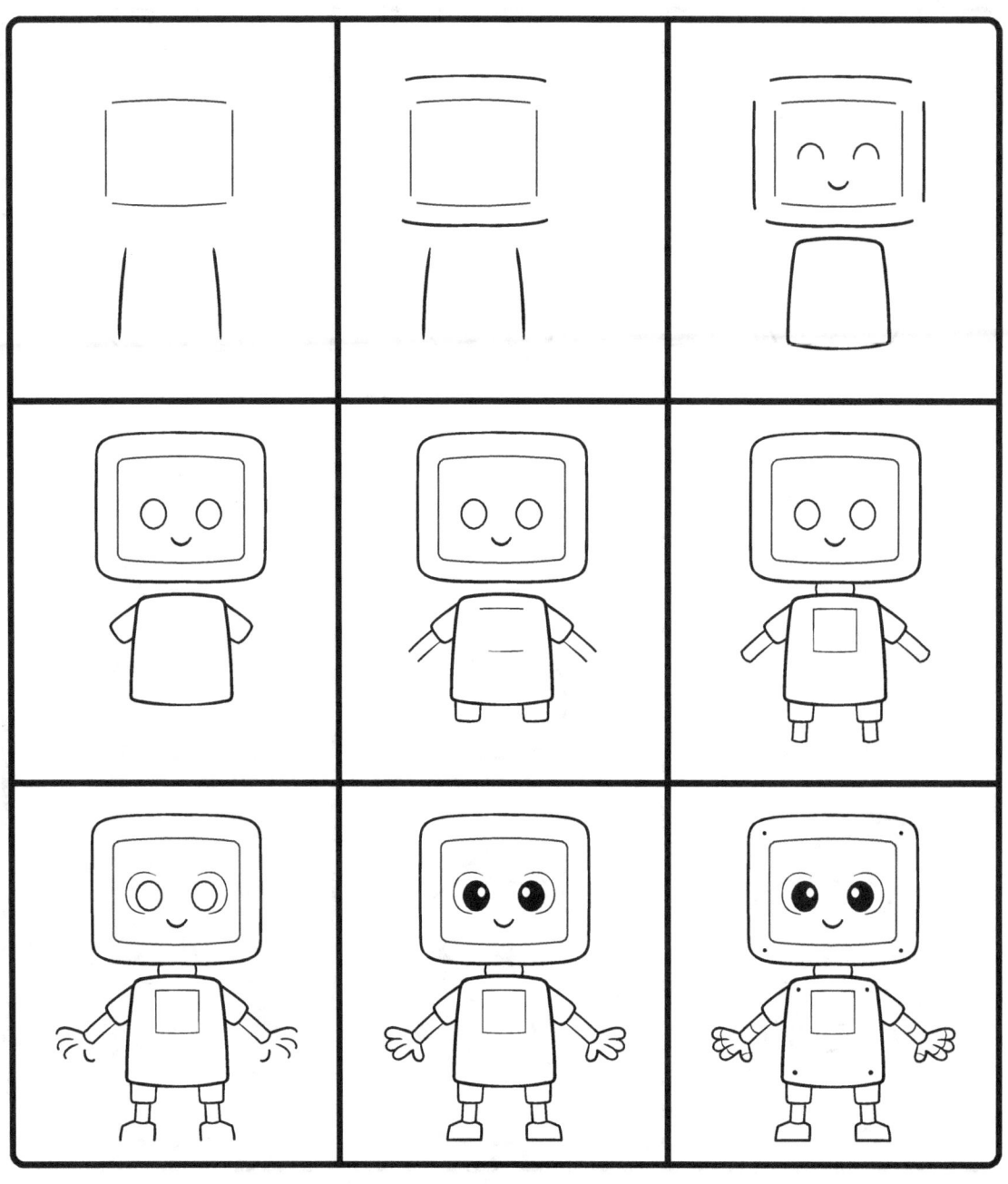

HOW TO DRAW DINOSAURS
35

CORN-PIE

LIVES: ON A SHELF IN A GIRL'S BEDROOM.

LOVES: POPPING BUBBLE-WRAP WITH ITS HORN.

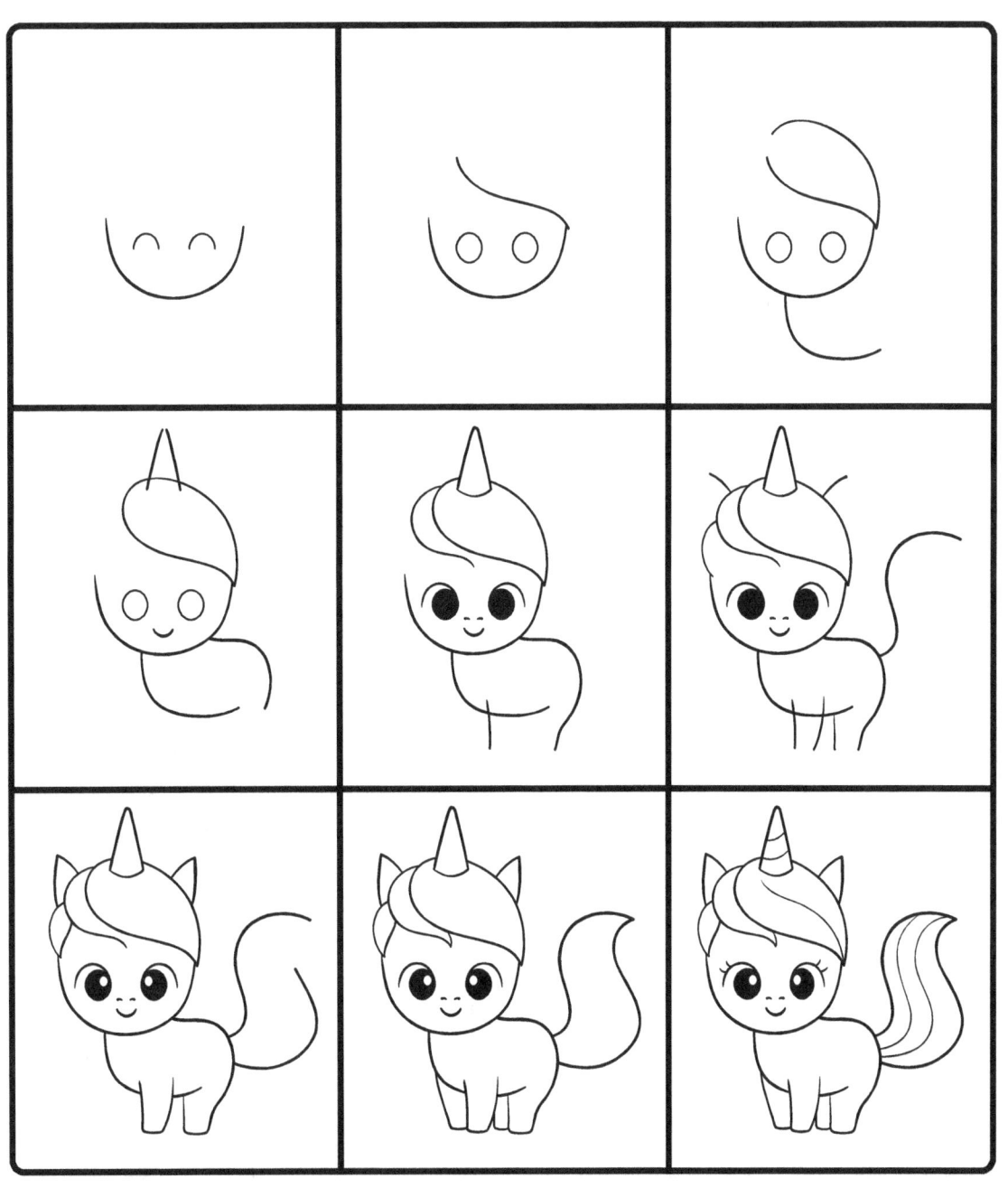

HOW TO DRAW DINOSAURS

MILKO

LIVES: IN A FAMILY'S FRIDGE.

LOVES: WHEN KIDS FLAVOR HIM WITH STRAWBERRY, BUT NOT BANANA, UGH!

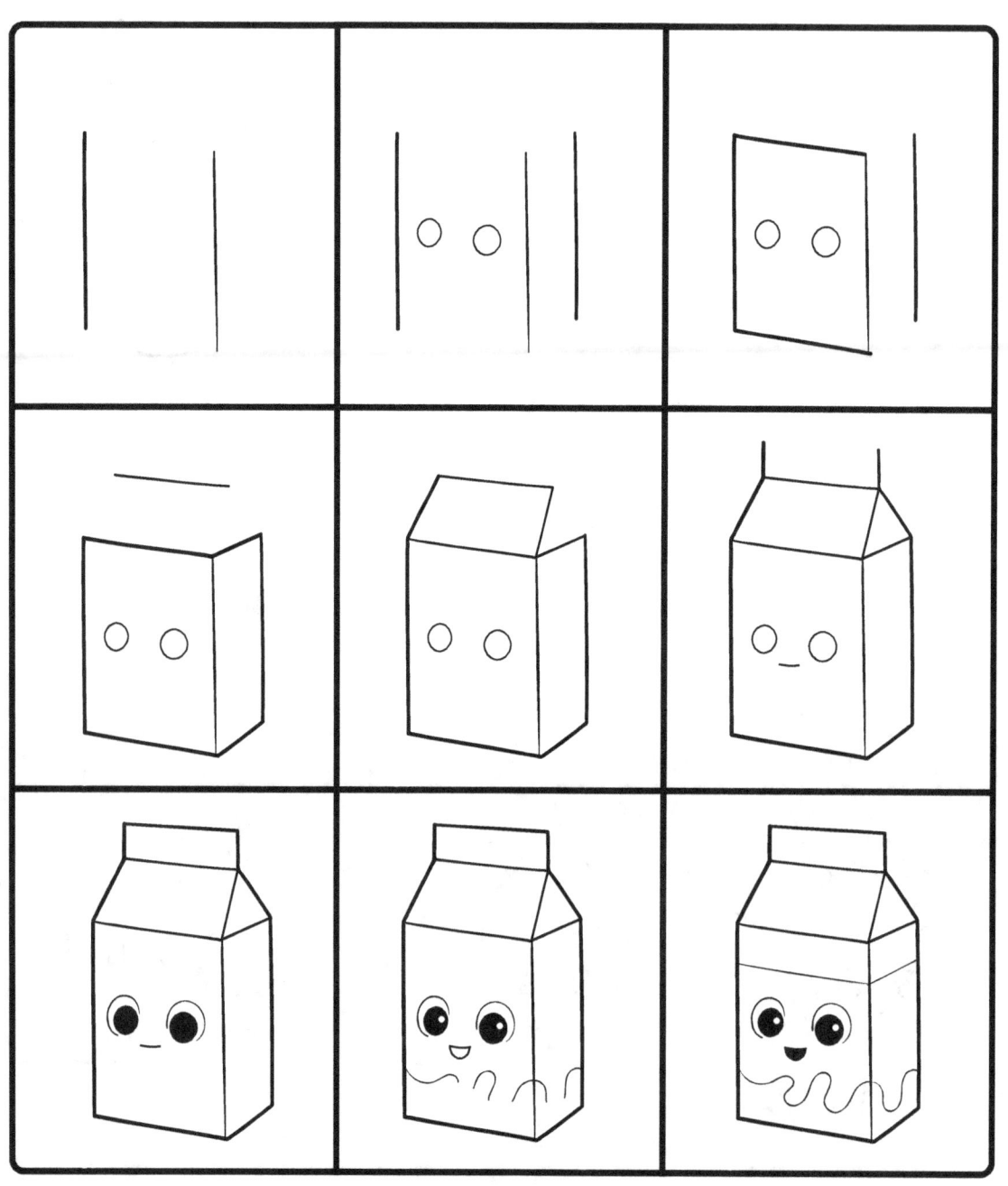

HOW TO DRAW DINOSAURS

BOTTBEE

LIVES: AT THE SUPERMARKET.

LOVES: THE THOUGHT OF BEING RECYCLED ONE DAY, BUT INTO A BIRD FEEDER OR A PLANT POT, NOT FLATTENED AND SQUISHED UP!

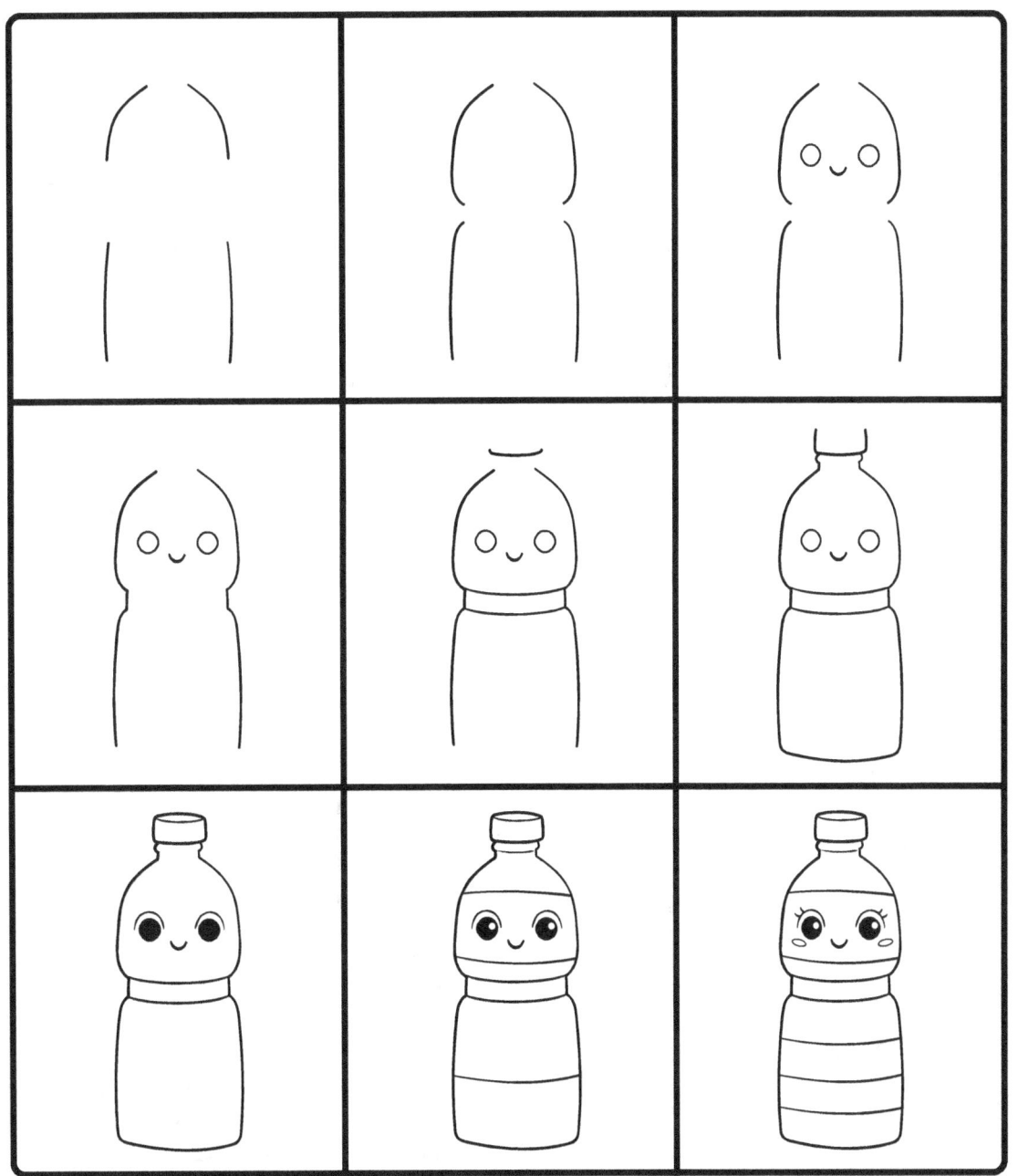

HOW TO DRAW DINOSAURS

SPRITE

LIVES: IN A GARDEN, OFTEN PASSED BY KIDS ON THEIR WAY TO SCHOOL.

LOVES: BEING BEAUTIFUL AND LIVING A LONG GREEN LIFE – DON'T PICK HER!

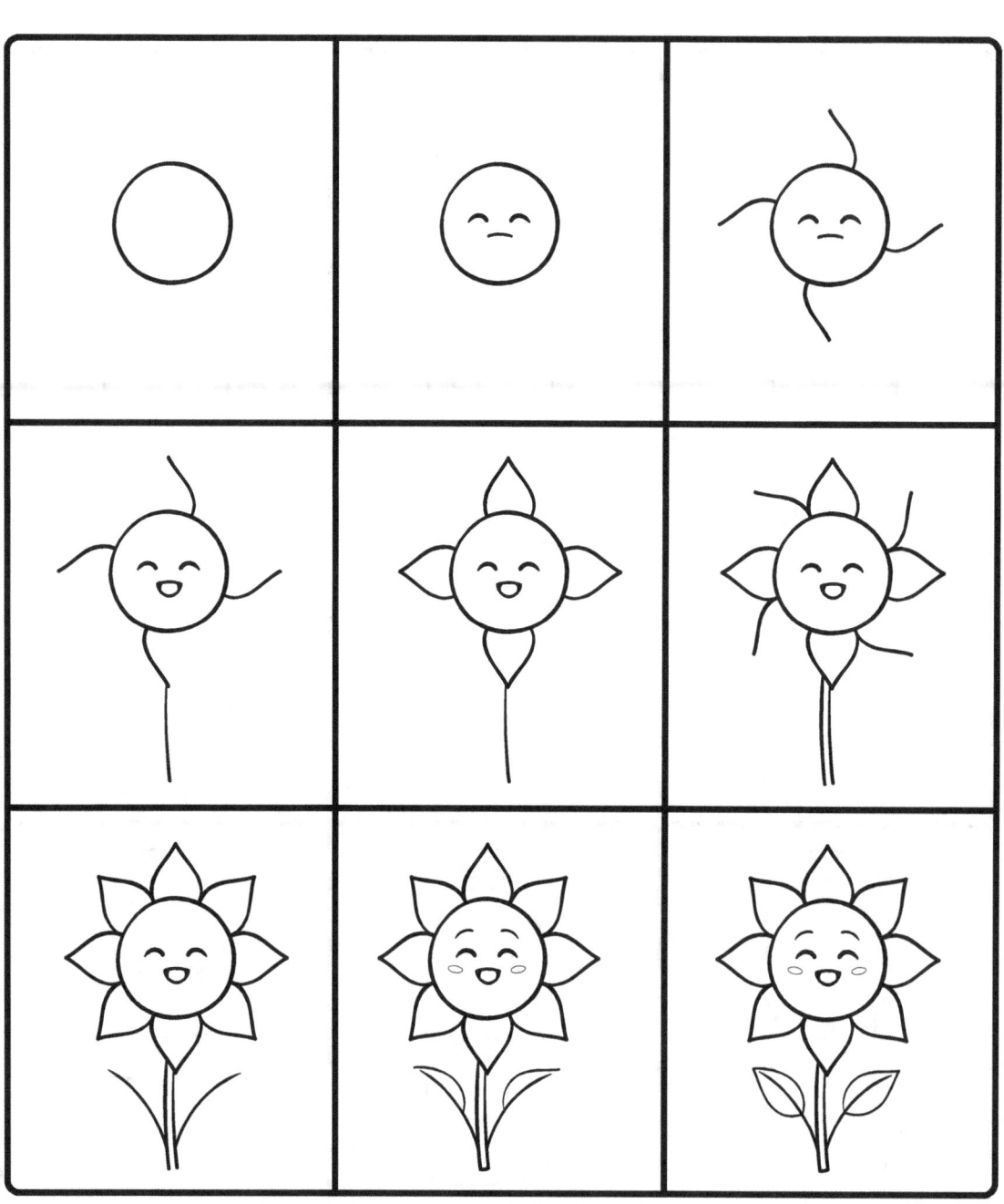

HOW TO DRAW DINOSAURS

CRUMBIE

LIVES: IN A CUPBOARD WAITING TO BE EATEN.

LOVES: THE BREEZE ON MY FROSTING WHEN THEY BLOW MY CANDLES AND MAKE A WISH.

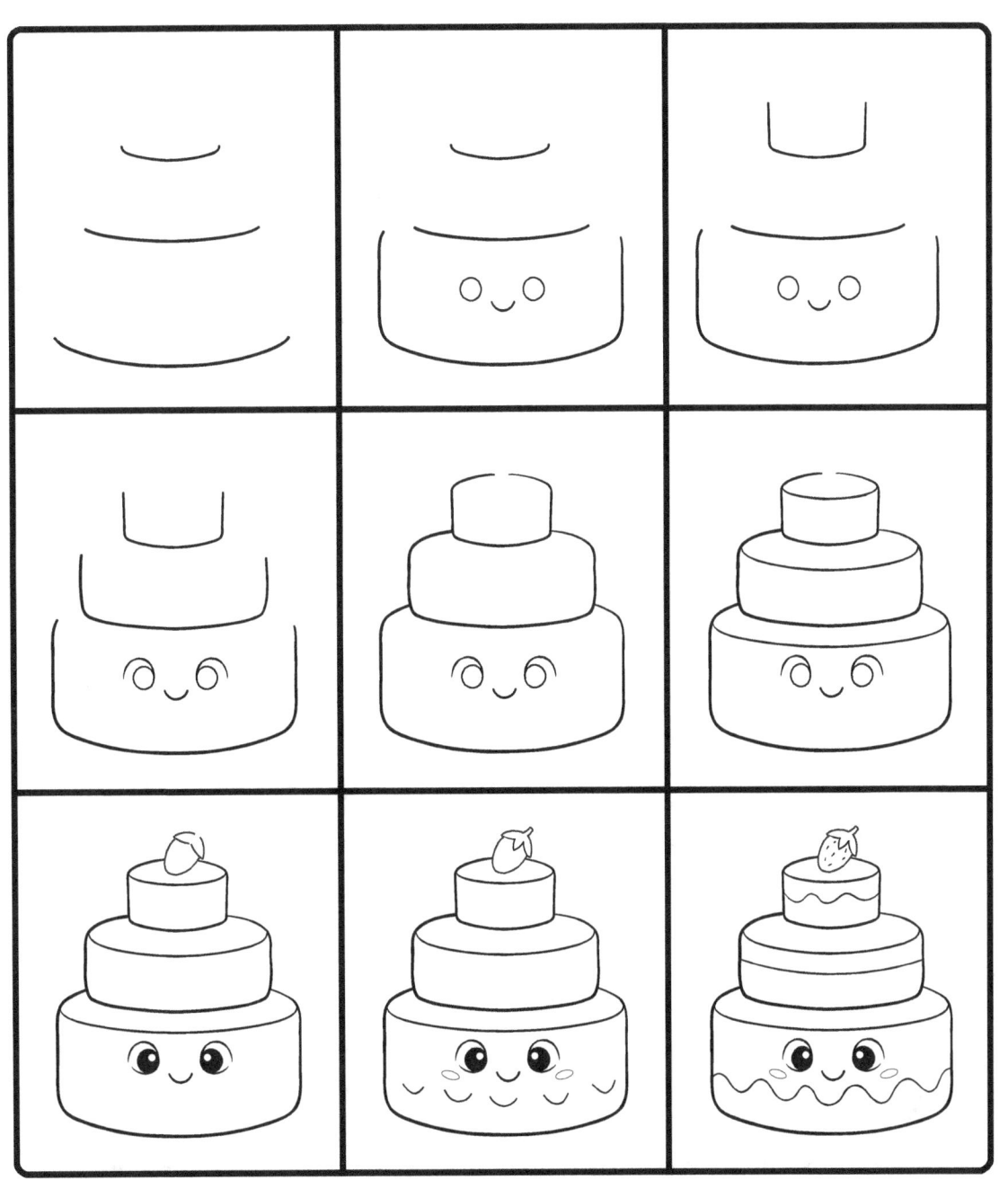

CHUTIE-CUTIE

LIVES: IN A BAKERY.

LOVES: GOING TO BIRTHDAYS AND BEING THE STAR OF THE PARTY!

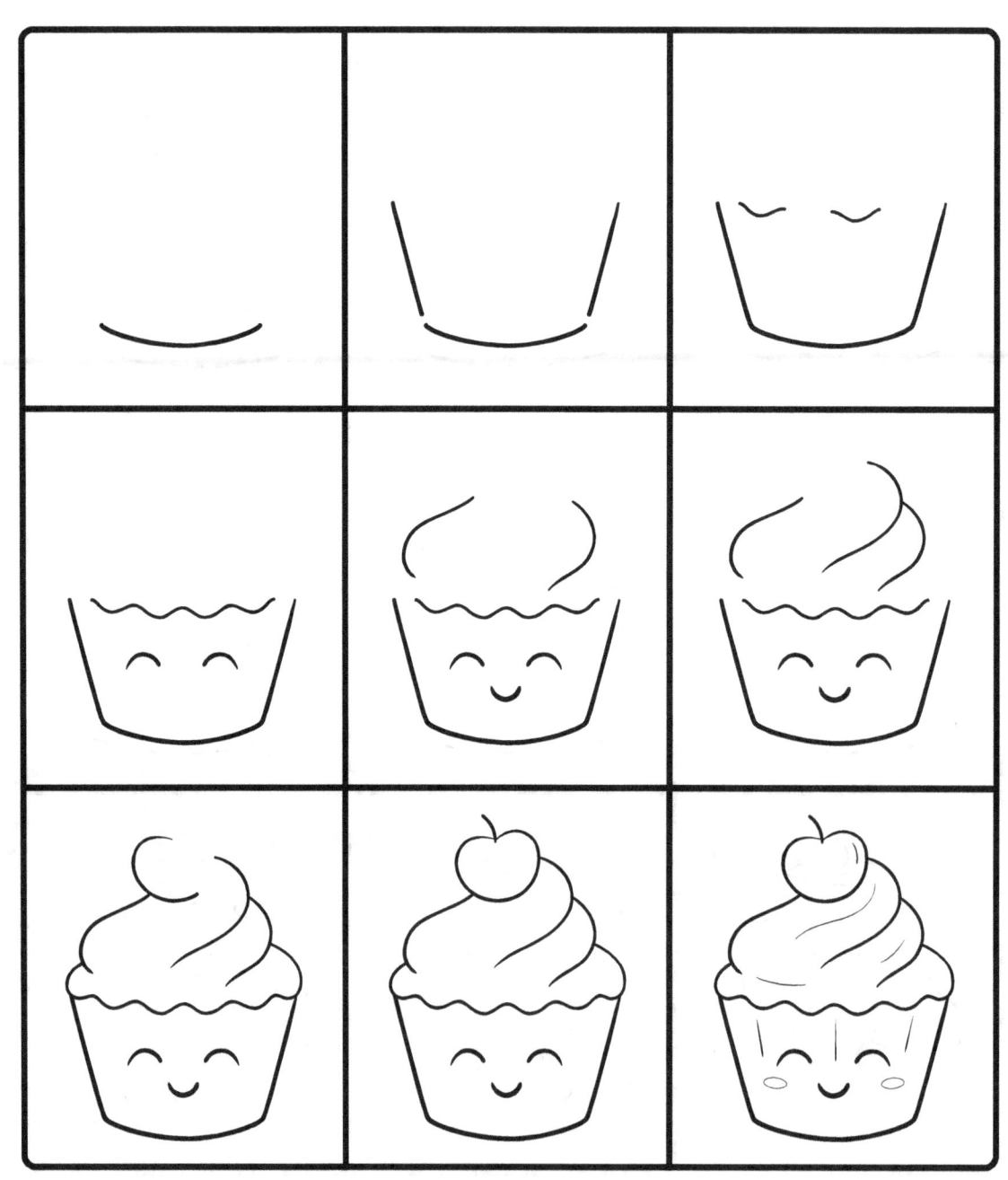

HOW TO DRAW DINOSAURS

DUDE

LIVES: IN A BASKET IN A TIKI HUT BY THE BEACH.

LOVES: BEING TURNED INTO A SUMMER DRINK, AND HOW THE STRAW TICKLES HIS BELLY!

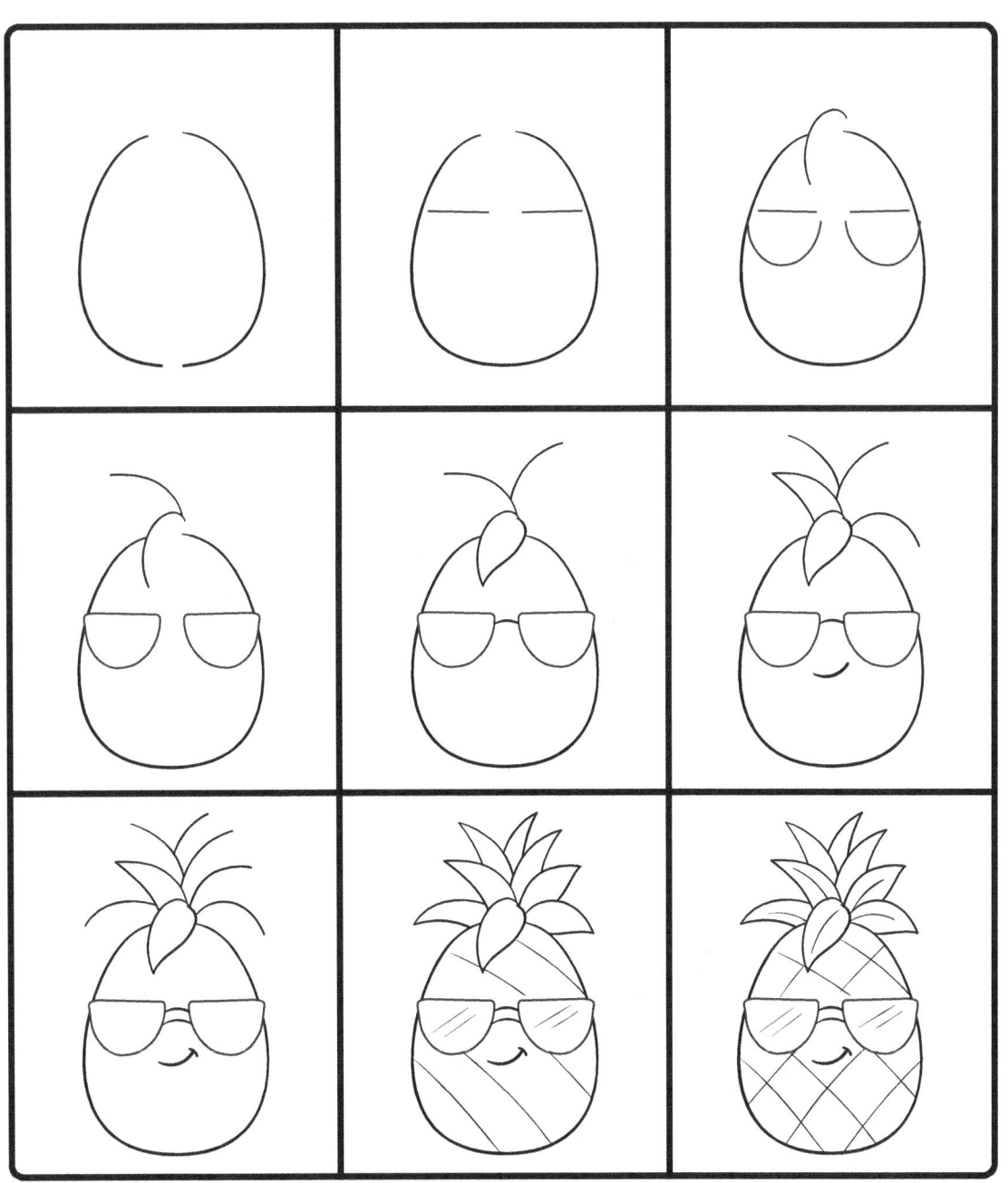

GREEN TIP

LIVES:
IN A SUNNY FIELD, SURROUNDED BY SUNFLOWERS AND BUTTERFLIES.

LOVES:
BEING MADE INTO A HALLOWEEN LANTERN AND LIGHTING UP THE PORCH.

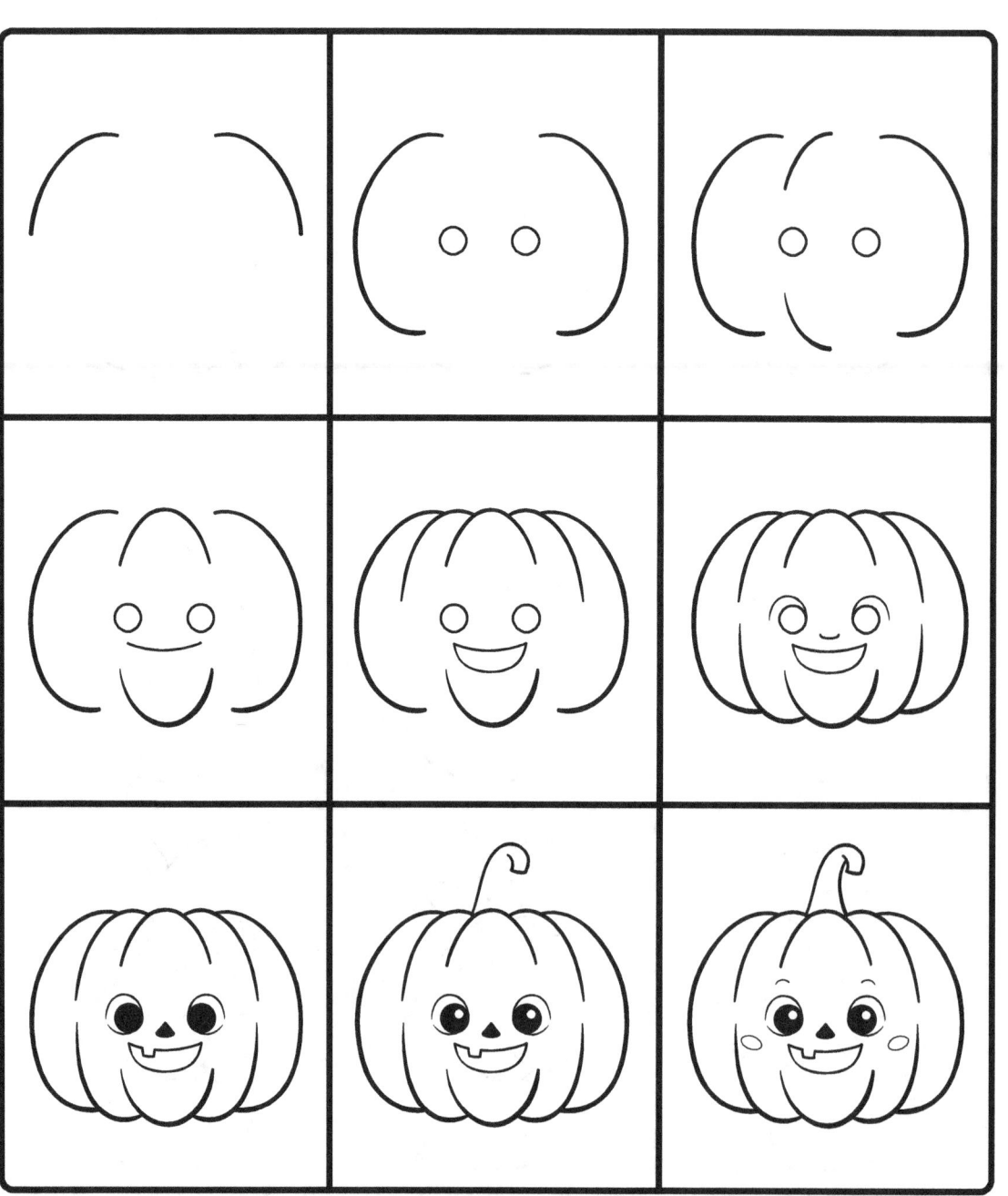

HOW TO DRAW DINOSAURS

SLURP

LIVES: IN A BOX IN THE GARAGE.

LOVES: BEING PUT IN A LUNCHBOX AND TAKEN TO SCHOOL – THERE IS SO MUCH TO LEARN!

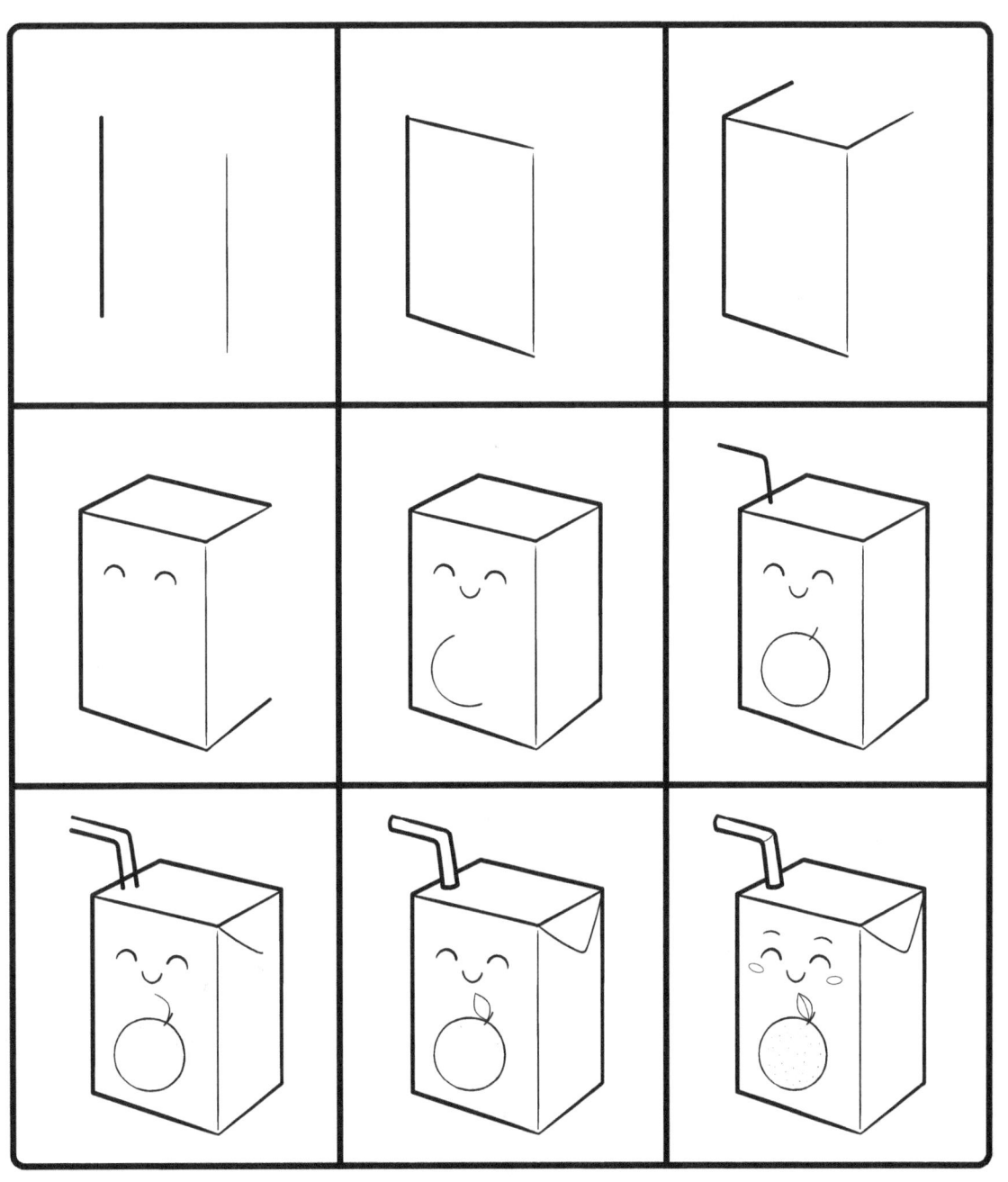

DASH

LIVES: UPSTAIRS FROM THE RESTAURANT HE WORKS IN.

LOVES: COOKING, IT'S SO EASY WITH AN INSTANT FLAME!

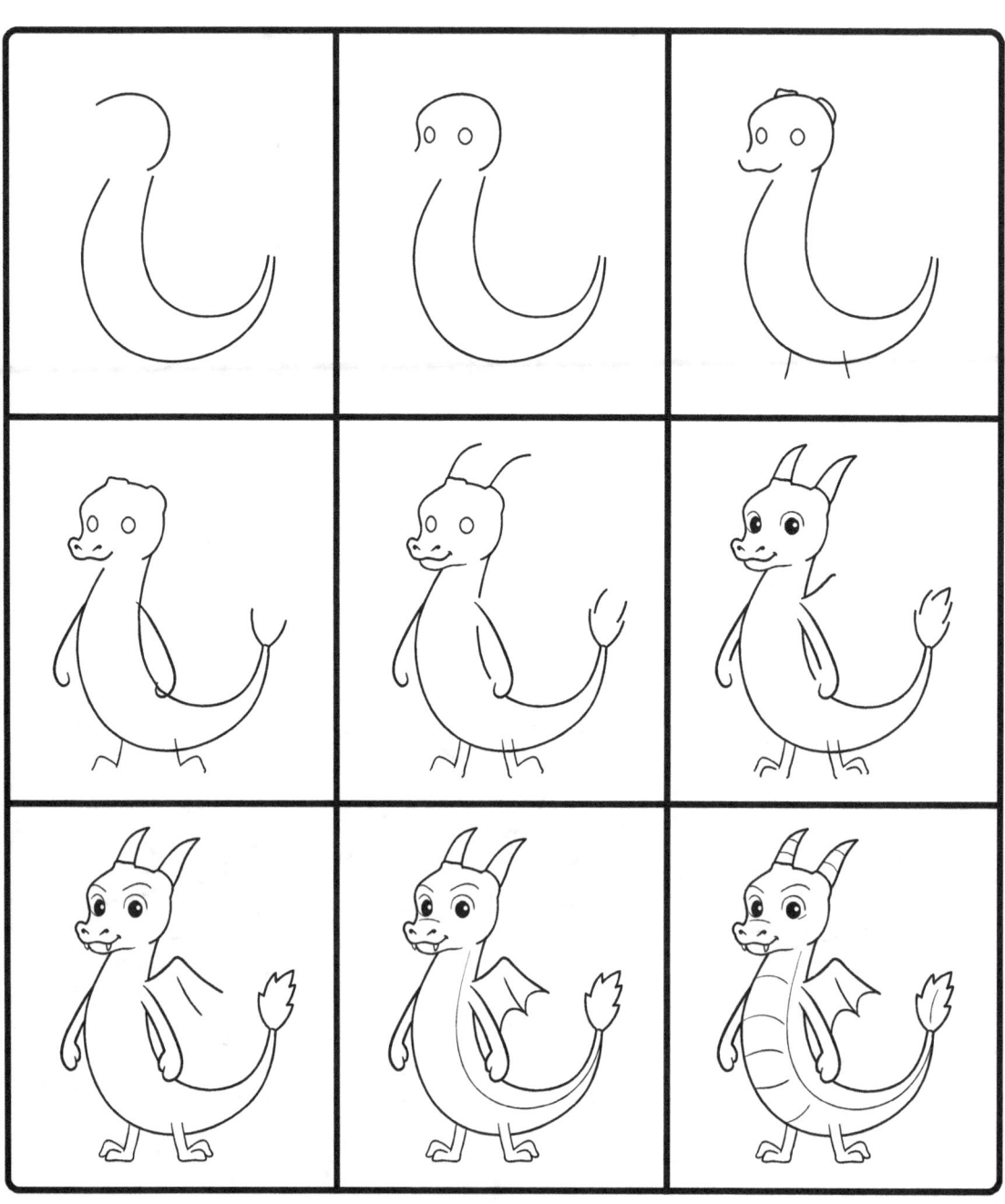

HOW TO DRAW DINOSAURS
45

SPLASH

LIVES:
IN THE ATLANTIC OCEAN.

LOVES:
BEING BIG AND BEAUTIFUL, BUT IT WOULD BE REALLY COOL TO BE ABLE TO CAMOUFLAGE LIKE SEAHORSES DO.

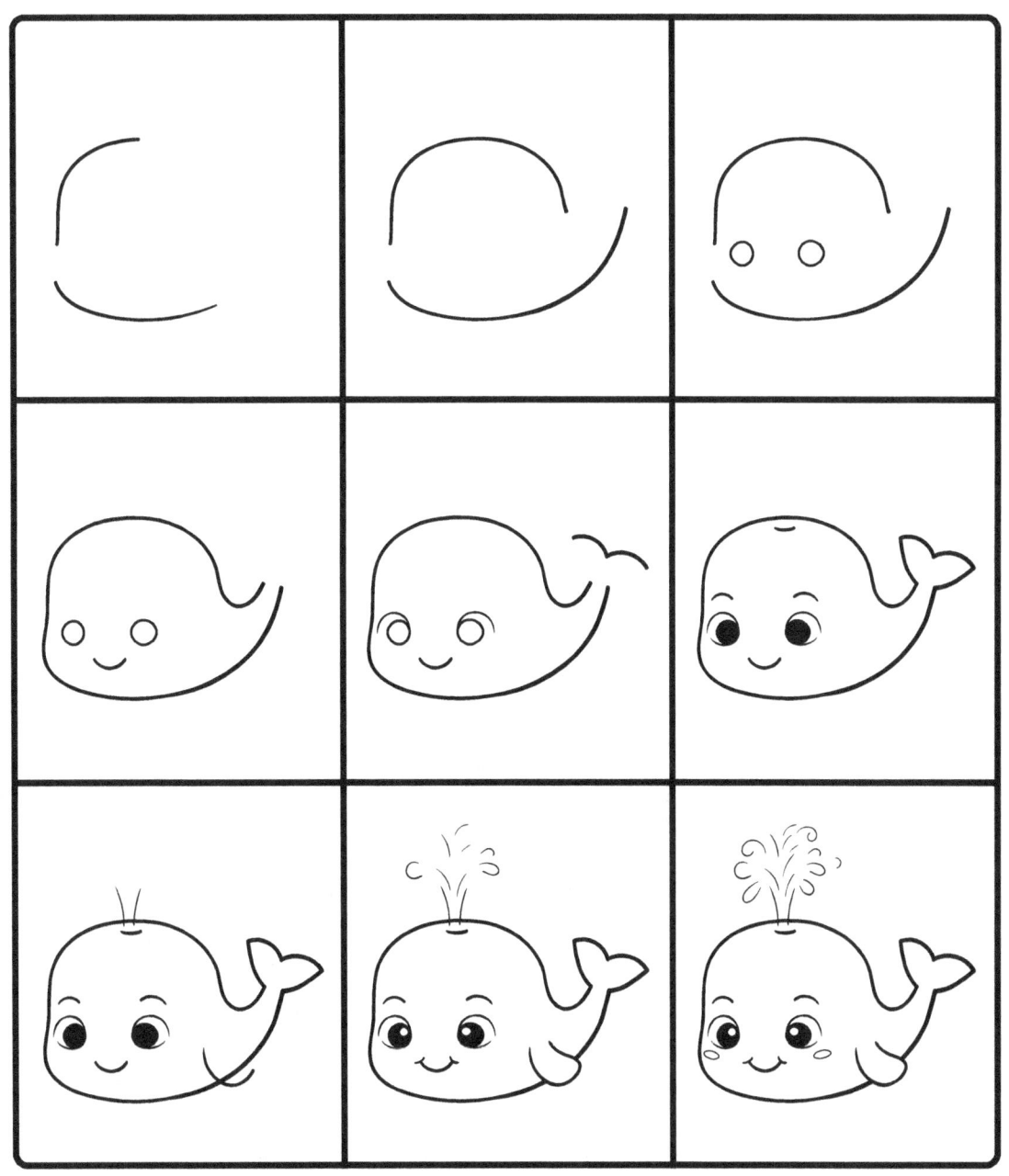

HOW TO DRAW DINOSAURS

SWISSY

LIVES: ON A FARM, SURROUNDED BY GREEN GRASS, COWS, AND A SHEEPDOG.

LOVES: THE SWISS ALPS, THE BEST PLACE IN THE WORLD!

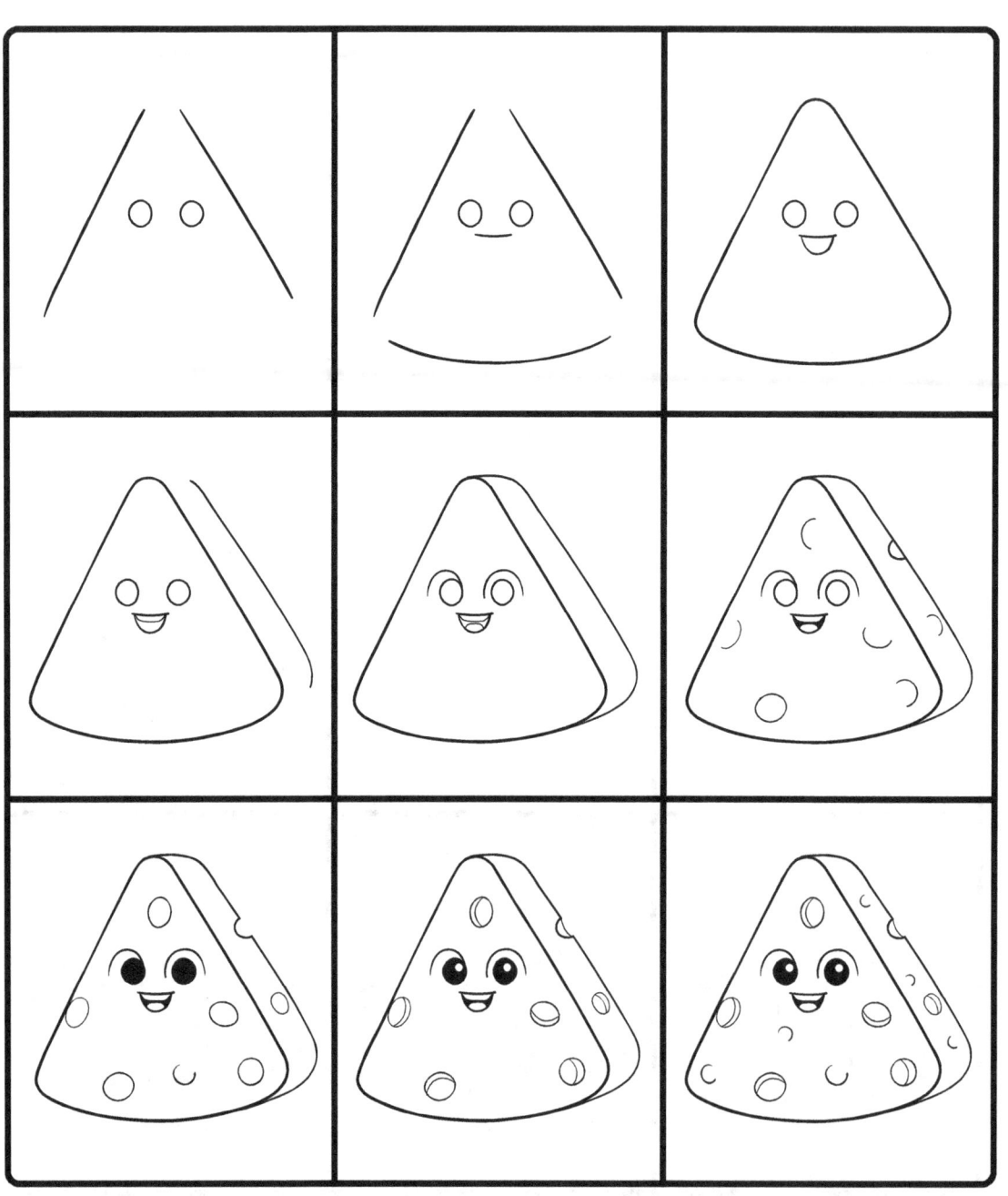

HOW TO DRAW DINOSAURS
47

LEGGY

LIVES: ON THE ROAD WITH HIS TRAVELING BAND.

LOVES: BEING ABLE TO PLAY SO MANY INSTRUMENTS AT ONCE!

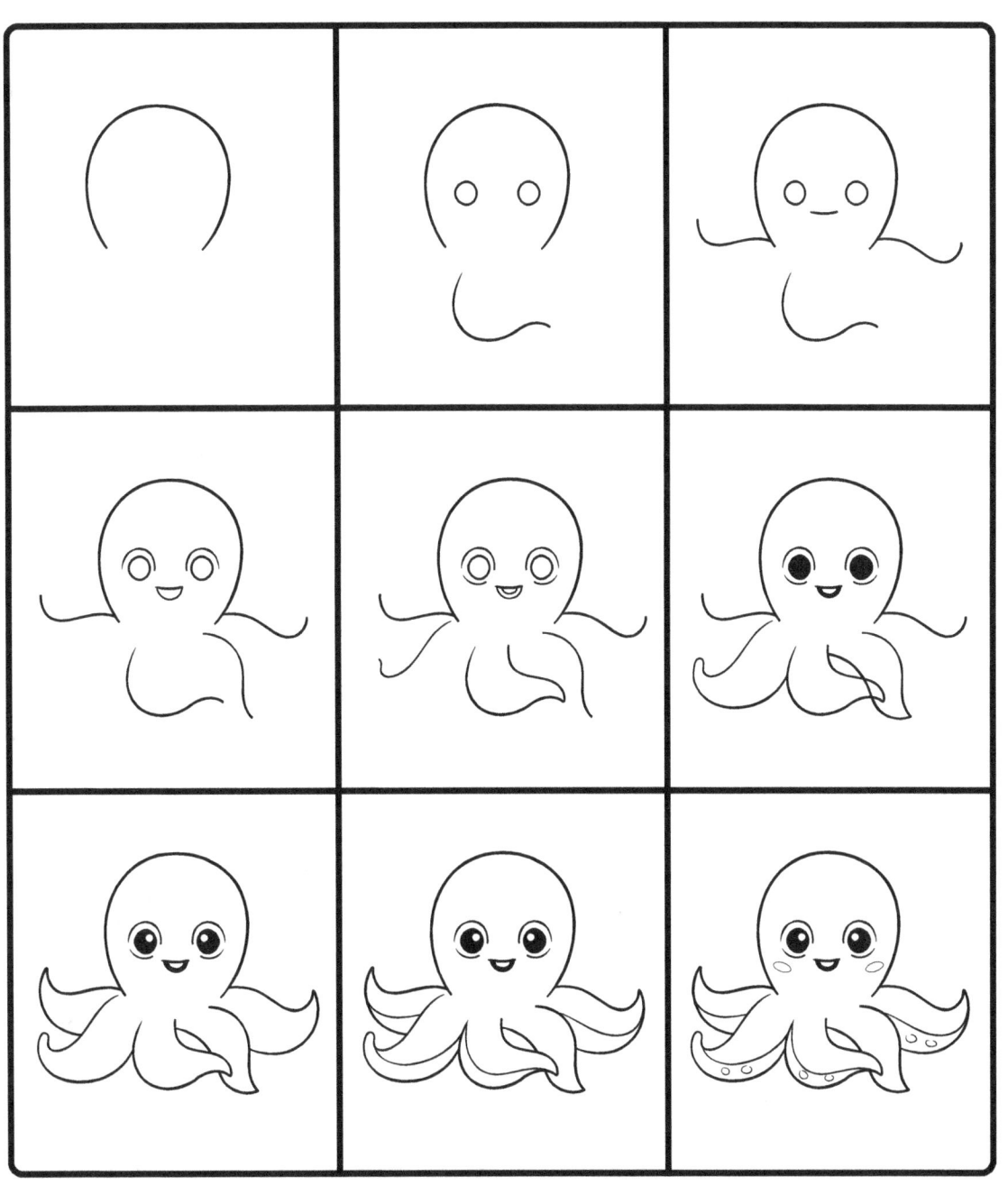

HOW TO DRAW DINOSAURS

PUNG

LIVES: IN THE NORTH POLE.

LOVES: ICESKATING WITH HER FRIENDS.

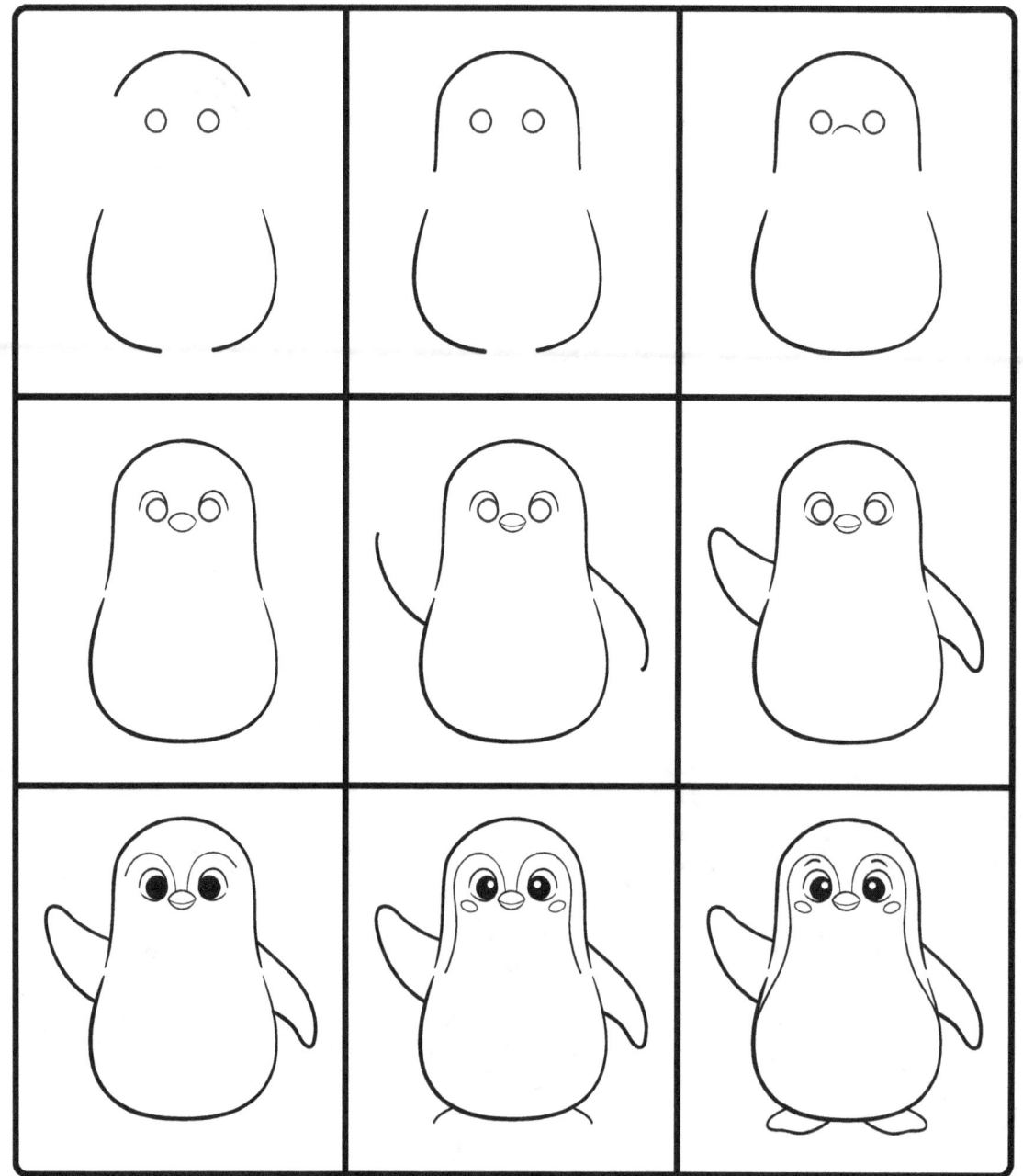

HOW TO DRAW DINOSAURS

49

BOXY

LIVES: IN A GIFT SHOP.

LOVES: WAITING UNDER THE TREE ON CHRISTMAS MORNING.

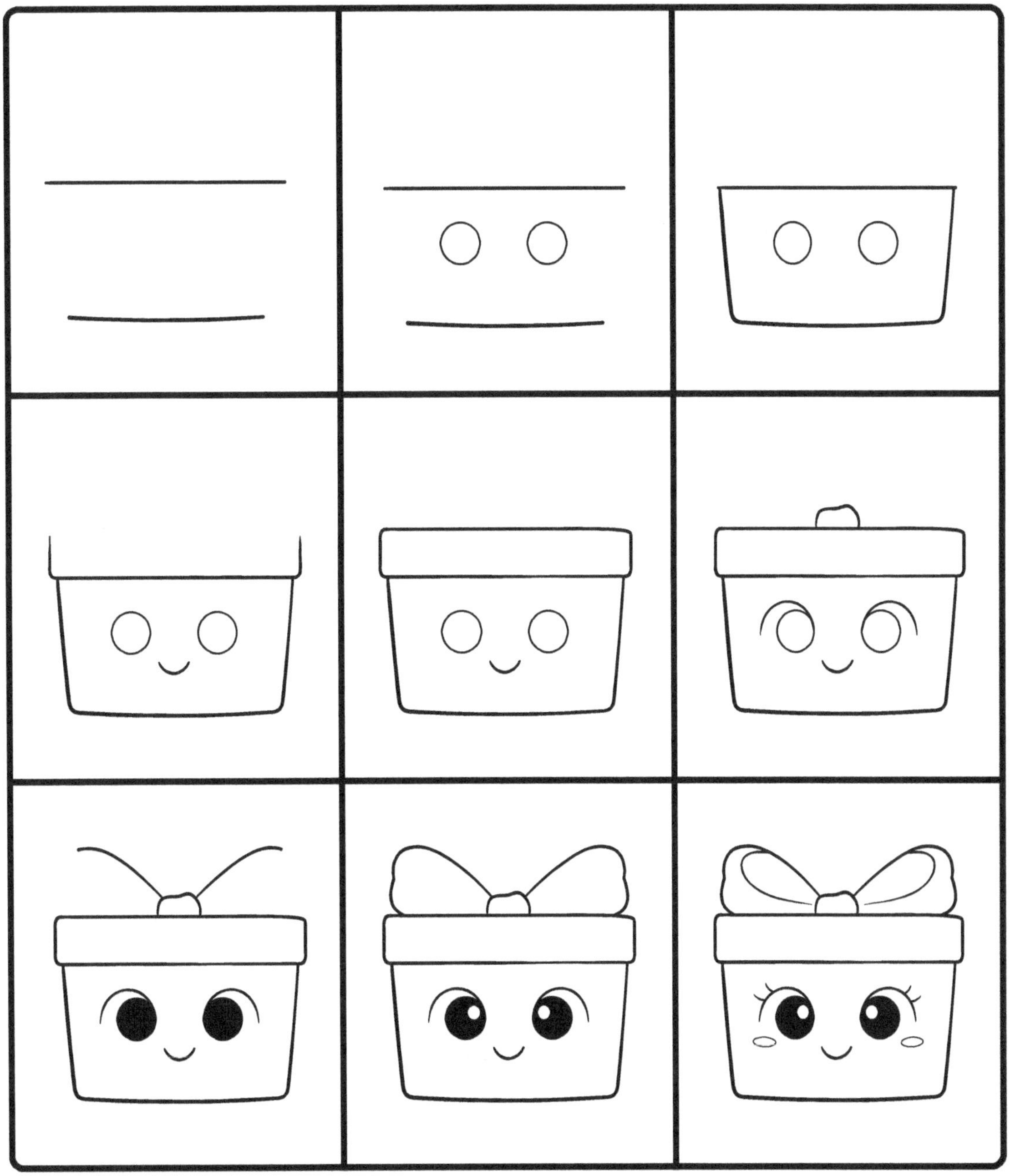

SPROUT

LIVES: AT A NURSERY.

LOVES: THE SAFETY OF LIVING IN A POT, BUT WOULD SO LOVE TO STRETCH ITS ROOTS OUT ONE DAY.

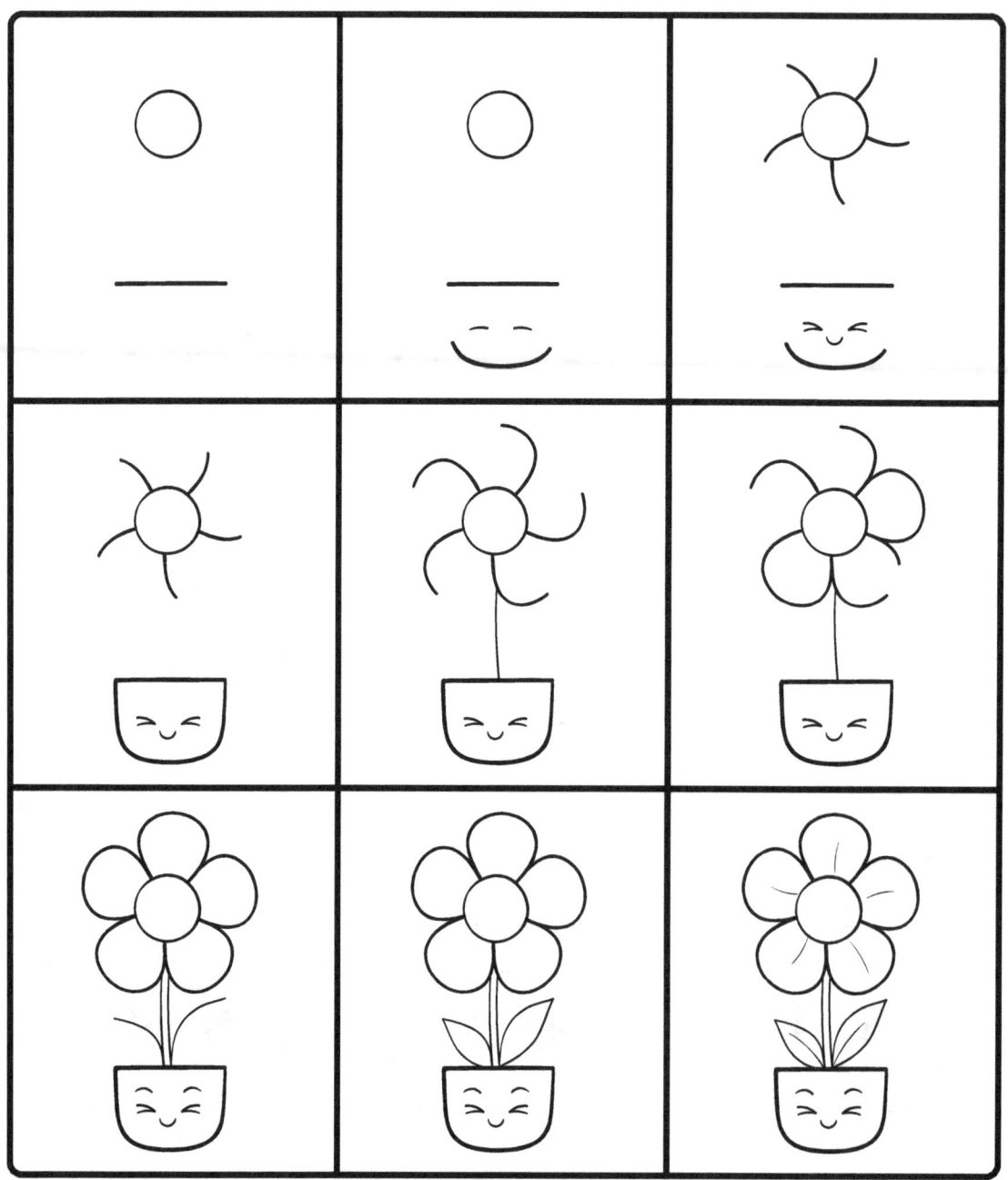

CHEEPER

LIVES: IN A CHOOK PEN IN A YARD.

LOVES: BEING LITTLE AND HELD IN SMALL WARM HANDS.

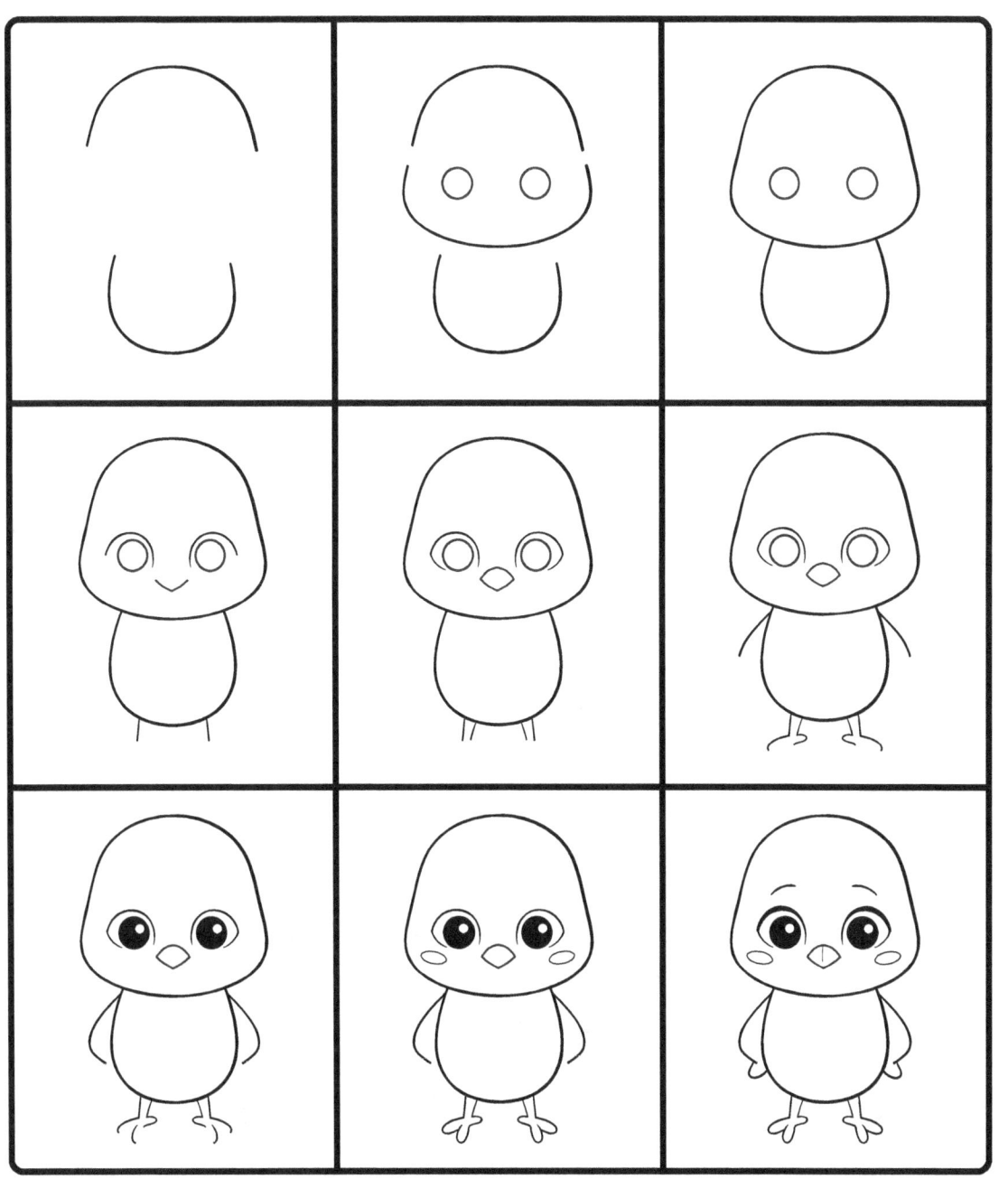

HOW TO DRAW DINOSAURS

CHUM

LIVES: IN A REMOTE FOREST.

LOVES: THE IDEA OF BEING IN THE CHIPMUNK BAND IN THE BIG CITY.

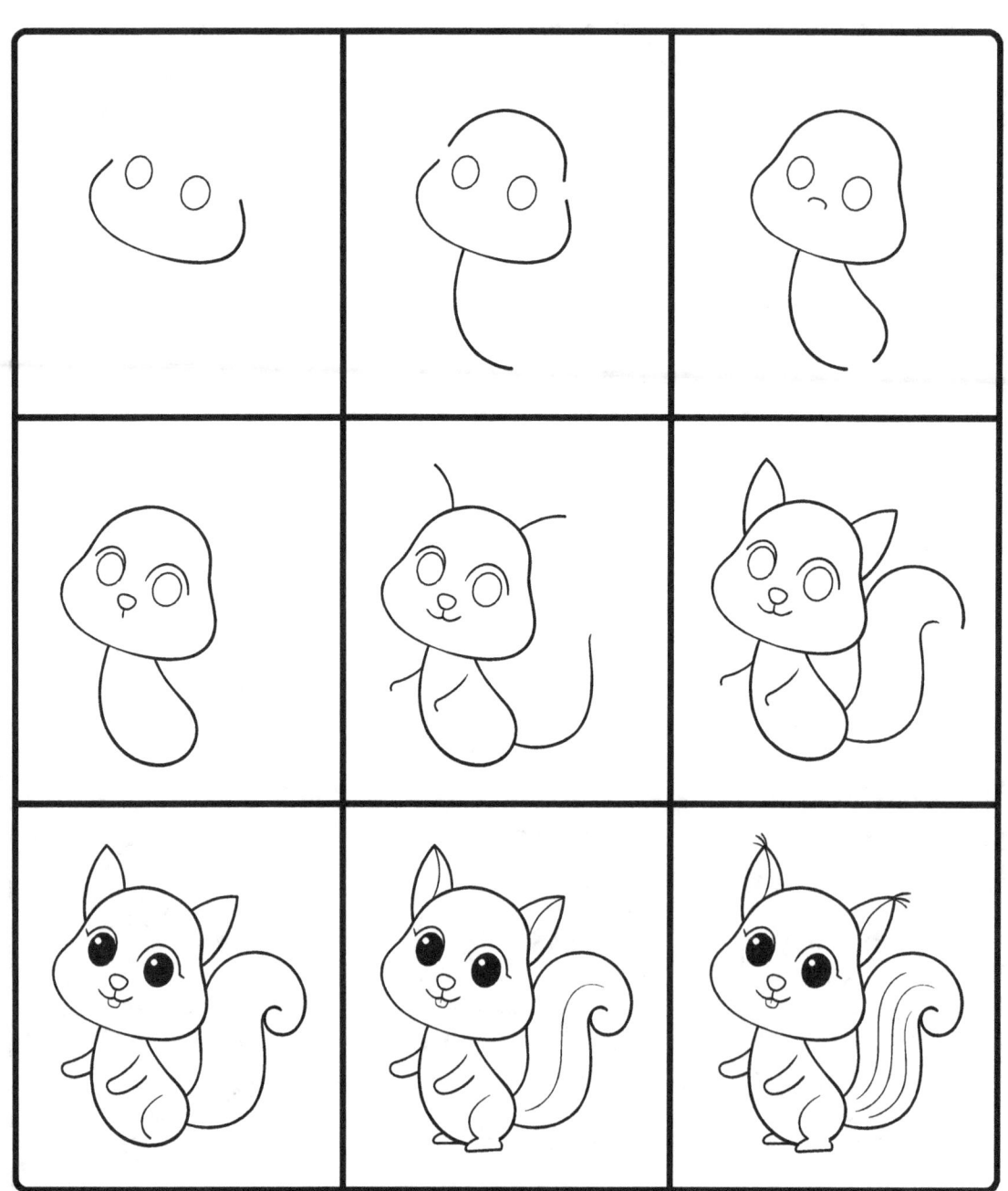

HOW TO DRAW DINOSAURS

SWIRL

LIVES: ON A SUPERMARKET SHELF.

LOVES: ROLLING OVER SUGAR AND CINNAMON, SO SWEET!

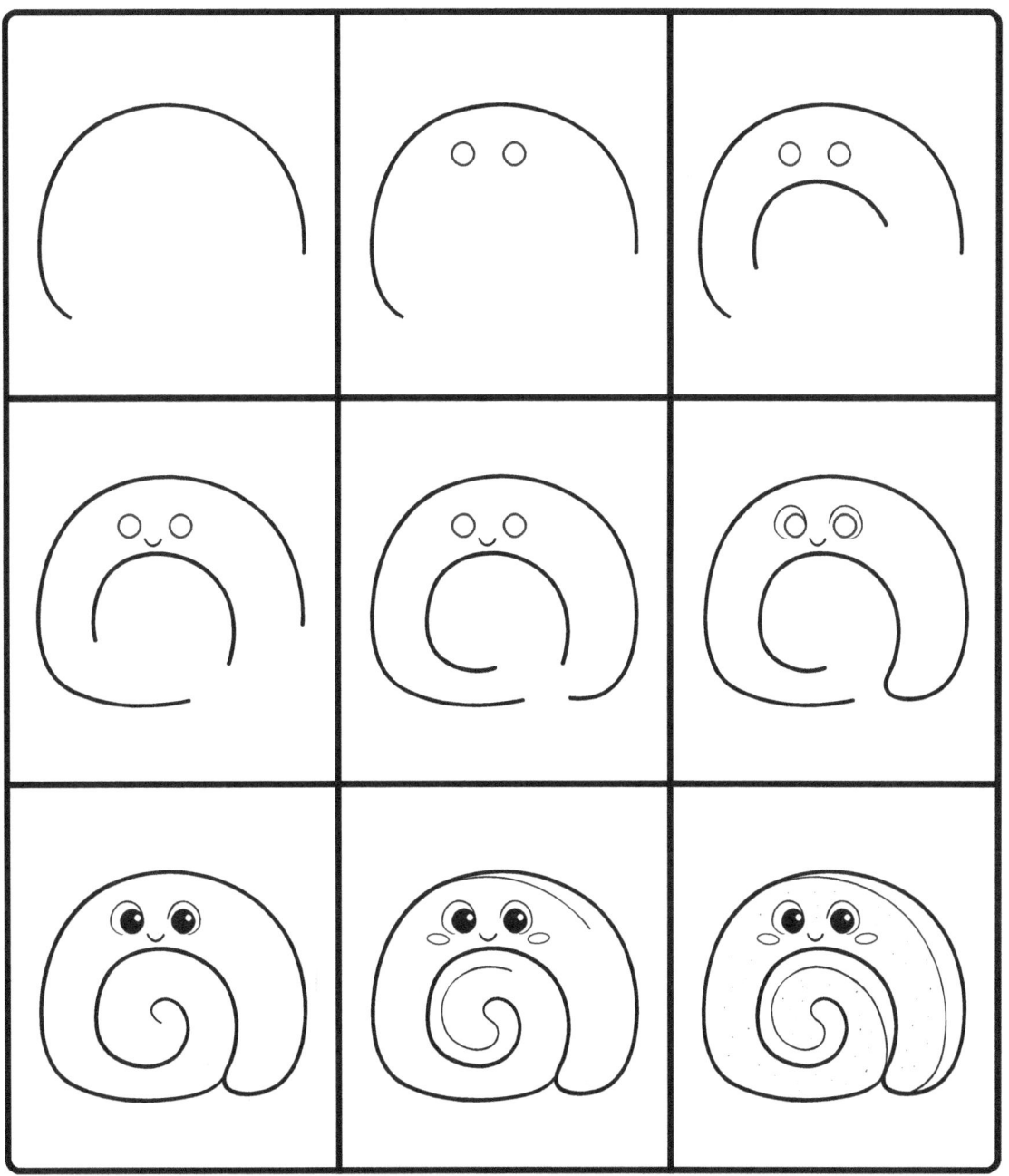

HOW TO DRAW DINOSAURS
54

NOO-NOO

LIVES: IN A RAMEN SHOP IN DOWNTOWN TOKYO.

LOVES: BEING SLURPED! AND CAN'T UNDERSTAND WHY IN SOME COUNTRIES IT'S RUDE TO SLURP!

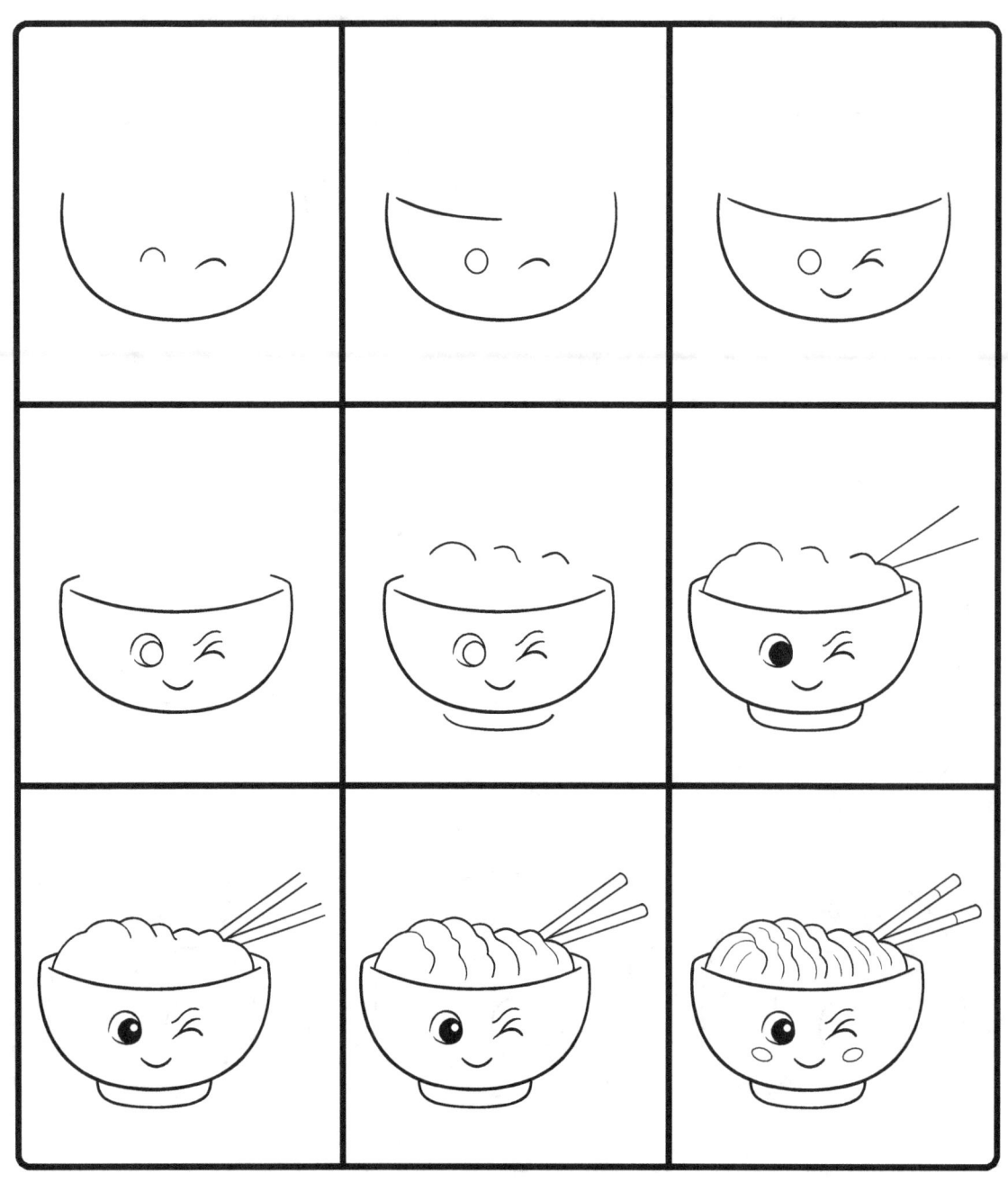

HOW TO DRAW DINOSAURS

CONCLUSION

SO HOW DID YOU GO DRAWING THE CHIBI CHARACTERS? WERE SOME TRICKIER THAN OTHERS? OR SOME MORE FUN TO DRAW?

NOW THAT YOU KNOW THE BASICS OF DRAWING EACH CHIBI, YOU CAN ADD YOUR OWN UNIQUE TOUCHES AND PERSONALITIES TO THEM!

IF YOU ENJOYED THE BOOK, PLEASE BE SURE TO LEAVE US A REVIEW ON AMAZON AS IT REALLY HELPS US GROW!

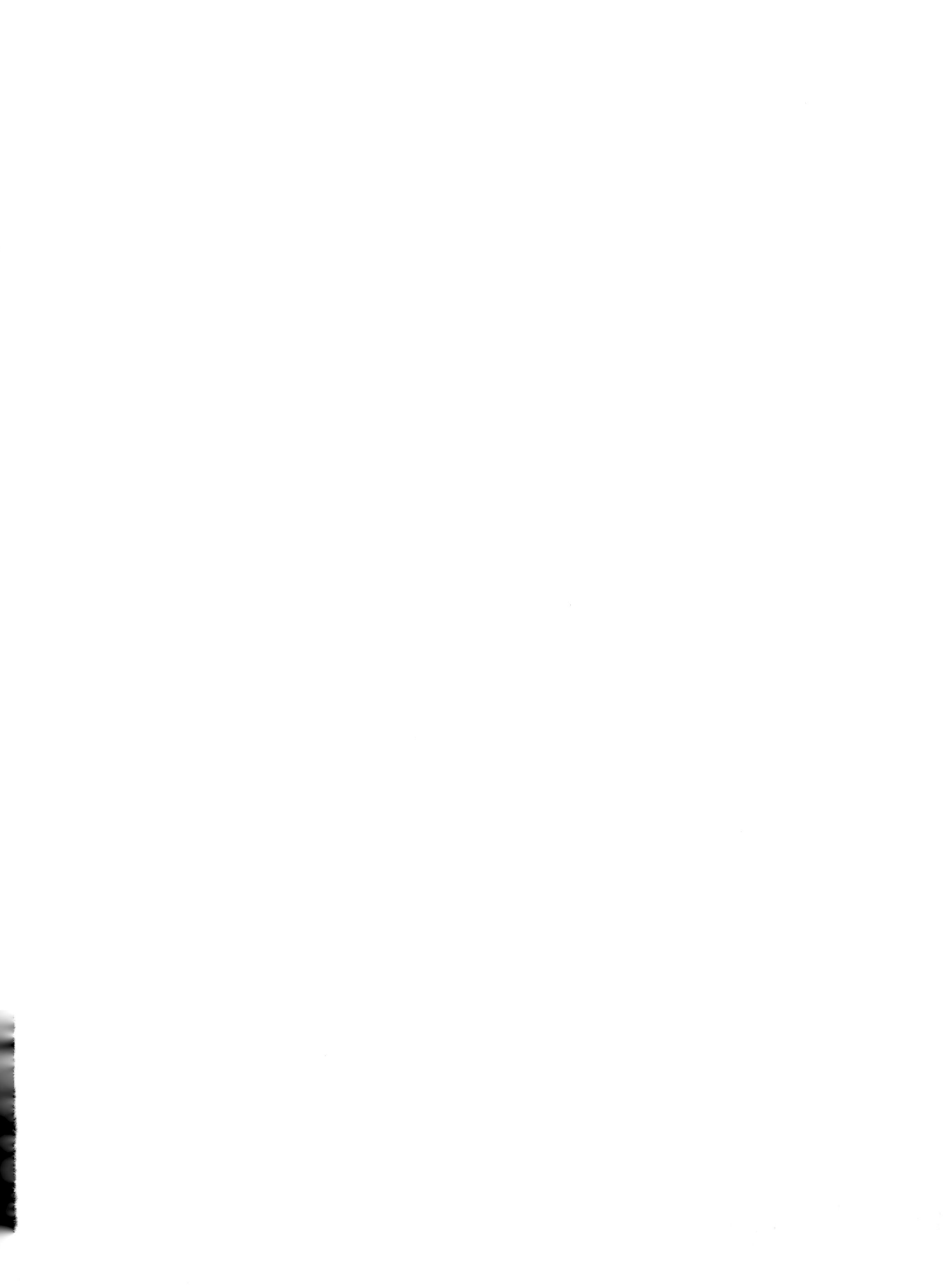

www.ingramcontent.com/pod-product-compliance
Lightning Source LLC
Chambersburg PA
CBHW080533220526
45465CB00006B/2697